Learning UML

Other resources from O'Reilly

Related titles	UML in a Nutshell	C++ in a Nutshell
	UML Pocket Reference	Java in a Nutshell

oreilly.com   *oreilly.com* is more than a complete catalog of O'Reilly books. You'll also find links to news, events, articles, weblogs, sample chapters, and code examples.

oreillynet.com is the essential portal for developers interested in open and emerging technologies, including new platforms, programming languages, and operating systems.

Conferences   O'Reilly & Associates brings diverse innovators together to nurture the ideas that spark revolutionary industries. We specialize in documenting the latest tools and systems, translating the innovator's knowledge into useful skills for those in the trenches. Visit *conferences.oreilly.com* for our upcoming events.

Safari Bookshelf (*safari.oreilly.com*) is the premier online reference library for programmers and IT professionals. Conduct searches across more than 1,000 books. Subscribers can zero in on answers to time-critical questions in a matter of seconds. Read the books on your Bookshelf from cover to cover or simply flip to the page you need. Try it today with a free trial.

Learning UML

Sinan Si Alhir

O'REILLY®

Beijing · Cambridge · Farnham · Köln · Paris · Sebastopol · Taipei · Tokyo

Learning UML
by Sinan Si Alhir

Copyright © 2003 O'Reilly & Associates, Inc. All rights reserved.
Printed in the United States of America.

Published by O'Reilly & Associates, Inc., 1005 Gravenstein Highway North, Sebastopol, CA 95472.

O'Reilly & Associates books may be purchased for educational, business, or sales promotional use. Online editions are also available for most titles (*safari.oreilly.com*). For more information, contact our corporate/institutional sales department: (800) 998-9938 or *corporate@oreilly.com*.

Editor:	Jonathan Gennick
Production Editor:	Mary Brady
Cover Designer:	Emma Colby
Interior Designer:	David Futato

Printing History:

July 2003:	First Edition.

ISBN: 0-596-00344-7
[C]

*This book is dedicated to
my wife, Milad, and my daughter, Nora,
whose love of learning is truly immeasurable.*

—Sinan Si Alhir

Table of Contents

Part III. Behavioral Modeling

Part IV. Beyond the Unified Modeling Language

Part V. Appendixes

Preface

Learning UML is the quintessential tutorial for the Unified Modeling Language (UML). The Unified Modeling Language is a language for communicating about systems: an evolutionary, general-purpose, broadly applicable, tool-supported, and industry-standardized modeling language for specifying, visualizing, constructing, and documenting the artifacts of a system-intensive process.

The UML was originally conceived by, and evolved primarily from, Rational Software Corporation and three of its most prominent methodologists, the *Three Amigos*: Grady Booch, James Rumbaugh, and Ivar Jacobson. The UML emerged as a standard from the Object Management Group (OMG) and Rational Software Corporation to unify the information systems and technology industry's best engineering practices as a collection of modeling techniques.

The UML may be applied to different types of systems (software and non-software), domains (business versus software), and methods or processes. The UML enables and promotes (but does not require nor mandate) a use-case-driven, architecture-centric, iterative and incremental, and risk-confronting process that is object-oriented and component-based. However, the UML does not prescribe any particular system development approach. Rather, it is flexible and can be customized to fit any method.

The UML is significantly more than a standard or another modeling language. It is a "paradigm," "philosophy," "revolution," and "evolution" of how we approach problem solving and systems. It is often said that the English language is the world's "universal language"; now it is virtually certain that the UML will be the information systems and technology world's "universal language."

Audience

This book is for anyone interested in learning and effectively and successfully applying the UML, including analysts and end users who specify requirements, architects who broadly design systems that satisfy requirements, designers who detail designs, developers who implement designs, testers who verify and validate systems against requirements, managers (portfolio, product, program, and project) who orchestrate system development efforts, and others involved in system development. No specific prior knowledge or skills are assumed; however, familiarity with object-oriented concepts may be of benefit.

Using This Book

While other tutorials focus on teaching you about the UML or some pseudomethodology or process that uses the UML, this one focuses on teaching you the essentials. It shows how to effectively and successfully apply the UML, including coverage of object orientation, common usage guidance, and suggestions on how to model systems. Each chapter uses an example-driven approach to progressively introduce key UML concepts with increasingly more involved examples. A project-management system case study is elaborated throughout the book, guiding you in learning how to read, understand, write, and effectively and successfully apply the UML. The objective is *not* to create a "complete" or "comprehensive" design from which to implement the system, but to explore the case study and to learn how to effectively and successfully apply the UML to communicate in real-world system development. Exercises are included so that you can practice and improve your skills.

When you are done reading this book, you will understand how to use the various UML diagrams and their elements based upon what you want to communicate and what each diagram emphasizes rather than based upon some pseudomethodology or process. You will also have gained insight into the rationale behind the language and how different pieces of the language fit together rather than be left with the perception that the UML is a hodgepodge of different types of diagrams without any underlying scheme, so that you'll generally be able to more effectively and successfully apply the UML. Such an understanding will allow you to stay abreast of the UML as it evolves and new versions become available.

This book, just like every other book ever written, is a snapshot of thoughts in time. The UML will most likely have evolved since the writing of this book; however, this book captures the foundation for learning and effectively and successfully applying the UML. Therefore, this book should remain valuable to you.

Organization and Content

This book consists of 5 parts, 10 chapters, and 2 appendixes.

Part I, *Fundamentals*, introduces the UML and object-oriented modeling. These chapters focus on *why* the UML is as it is and *what* each part is used for.

Chapter 1, *Introduction*
   Introduces the UML.

Chapter 2, *Object-Oriented Modeling*
   Introduces the object-oriented paradigm and the UML's modeling techniques.

Part II, *Structural Modeling*, covers structural modeling and focuses on *how* the UML is used for modeling the elements that make up a system and their relationships.

Chapter 3, *Class and Object Diagrams*
   Shows you how to model the structure of a system in general and at a particular point in time using class and object diagrams, respectively.

Chapter 4, *Use-Case Diagrams*
   Shows you how to model the functionality of a system using use-case diagrams.

Chapter 5, *Component and Deployment Diagrams*
   Shows you how to model the implementation and environment of a system, respectively.

Part III, *Behavioral Modeling*, covers behavioral modeling and focuses on *how* the UML is used for modeling the interactions and collaborations of the elements that make up a system.

Chapter 6, *Sequence and Collaboration Diagrams*
   Shows you how to model the behavior of elements that make up a system as they interact over time using sequence diagrams. It also shows you how to use collaboration diagrams to model behavior over time, and at the same time shows how the elements are related in space.

Chapter 7, *State Diagrams*
   Shows you how to model the lifecycle of elements that make up a system using state diagrams.

Chapter 8, *Activity Diagrams*
   Shows you how to model the activities and responsibilities of elements that make up a system using activity diagrams.

Part IV, *Beyond the Unified Modeling Language*, introduces other capabilities of the UML, including extending the language and capturing constraints or rules for model elements.

Chapter 9, *Extension Mechanisms*
   Allows you to understand the UML's extension mechanisms, and gives you a glimpse of some of the possibilities of applying the UML's extension mechanisms.

Chapter 10, *The Object Constraint Language*
   Introduces you to the UML's Object Constraint Language (OCL). You can reference other, OCL-specific books to learn more about the OCL.

Part V, *Appendixes*, contains supporting material.

Appendix A, *References*
> Offers references to notable resources on the World Wide Web and various books.

Appendix B, *Exercise Solutions*
> Offers solutions to the exercises.

This book does not contain any source code, because focus is given to the modeling language independent of any translation to a specific implementation. Rather than show you how to translate a system to a specific implementation, the focus is on learning and effectively and successfully applying the UML.

Conventions Used in This Book

This book uses the following typographic conventions:

Constant width
> Constant width is used for UML keywords, UML element names such as class and object names, method names and signatures, constraints, properties, and any other time text from a UML diagram that is referenced in the main body of the text.

Italic
> Italic is used for emphasis, for first use of a technical term, and for URLs.

...
> Ellipses indicate text in examples or UML diagrams that has been omitted for clarity.

 This icon indicates a tip, suggestion, or general note.

 This icon indicates a warning or caution.

Comments and Questions

We have tested and verified the information in this book to the best of our ability, but you may find that features have changed or that we have made mistakes. If so, please notify us by writing to:

O'Reilly & Associates
1005 Gravenstein Highway North
Sebastopol, CA 95472
800-998-9938 (in the U.S. or Canada)
707-829-0515 (international or local)
707-829-0104 (FAX)

You can also send messages electronically. To be put on the mailing list or request a catalog, send email to:

info@oreilly.com

To ask technical questions or comment on the book, send email to:

bookquestions@oreilly.com

We have an online catalog page for this book, where you can find examples and errata (previously reported errors and corrections are available for public view there). You can access this page at:

http://www.oreilly.com/catalog/learnuml

For more information about this book and others, see the O'Reilly web site:

http://www.oreilly.com

Readers who would like to contact the author to ask questions or to discuss this book, the UML, object orientation, or other related topics are very welcome to do so at the email address, *salhir@earthlink.net.* You may also visit the author's home page at *http://home.earthlink.net/~salhir.*

Acknowledgments

There are a number of individuals who made this work possible, specifically those who had to live with me, who demonstrated an abundance of encouragement, patience, understanding, and had to sacrifice a part of themselves to make this endeavor real.

I thank God for making everything possible, and I thank my family for what they have been, are, and will be—the essence of my world: my father Saad and mother Rabab, my brothers Ghazwan and Phillip, my wife Milad, and last but surely never least, my daughter, Nora.

I would also like to thank my mentors, Dr. Carl V. Page and Dr. George C. Stockman, for their continued and everlasting "presence" in my world.

In addition, I would like to thank the many practitioners leveraging my first book *UML in Nutshell* (O'Reilly) and my second book *Guide to Applying the UML* (Springer-Verlag) from across the world for their support and continued acknowledgment of their value.

I would also like to thank Tim O'Reilly for giving me the opportunity to do this book; my editor, Jonathan Gennick, for his effort and understanding and for showing me the true fabric that makes O'Reilly and Associates and *Learning* books a success; and all of the staff at O'Reilly and Associates for their work in bringing this book to life. Thanks also go to the following reviewers for their feedback: Don Bales, Peter Komisar, and John Whiteway.

I will not forget any of you, and I only ask that you please remember me.

PART I

Fundamentals

CHAPTER 1

Introduction

This chapter introduces the Unified Modeling Language (UML). I discuss why the UML is important and how one can learn it, by focusing on the object-oriented paradigm, structural modeling techniques, behavioral modeling techniques, and other capabilities of the UML. There are many good reasons to learn and use the UML. Quite simply, the UML is the lingua franca of the information systems and technology industry. More formally, the UML is a general-purpose and industry-standard language that is broadly applicable and well supported by tools in today's marketplace.

System development involves creating systems that satisfy requirements using a system development lifecycle process. Essentially, requirements represent problems to be addressed, a system represents a solution that addresses those problems, and system development is a problem-solving process that involves understanding the problem, solving the problem, and implementing the solution. Natural languages are used to communicate the requirements. Programming languages (and more broadly, technology-based implementation languages such as the Extensible Markup Language (XML), the Structured Query Language (SQL), Java, C#, and so forth) are used to communicate the details of the system. Because natural languages are less precise than programming languages, modeling languages (such as the UML) are used in a problem-solving process to bridge the chasm between the requirements and the system.

A general-purpose language such as the UML may be applied throughout the system-development process all the way from requirements gathering to implementation of the system. As a broadly applicable language, UML may also be applied to different types of systems, domains, and processes. Therefore, we can use the UML to communicate about software systems and non-software systems (often known as *business systems*) in various domains or industries such as manufacturing, banking, e-business, and so forth. Furthermore, we can apply the UML with any process or approach. It is supported by various tool vendors, industry-standardized, and not a proprietary or closed modeling language.

What Is the UML?

Quite simply, the UML is a visual language for modeling and communicating about systems through the use of diagrams and supporting text. For example, Figure 1-1 communicates the following:

- A manager leads a team that executes a project.
- Each manager has a name and phone number, and may initiate a project or terminate a project.
- Each project has a name, start date, and end date.
- Each team has a description, and that is all we are interested in concerning the team.

Don't worry if Figure 1-1 does not make complete sense. We will explore this figure and the UML in more detail in Chapter 2.

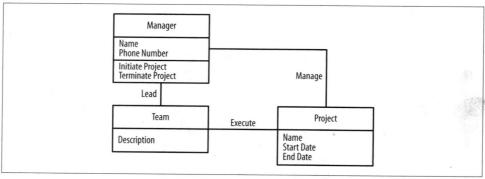

Figure 1-1. Managers, projects, and teams

The Three Aspects of UML

As you know by now, UML is an abbreviation for *Unified Modeling Language*. Each of these words speaks to an important aspect of the UML. The next few sections talk about these aspects, working through the words of the abbreviation in reverse order.

Language

A *language* enables us to communicate about a subject. In system development, the subject includes the requirements and the system. Without a language, it is difficult for team members to communicate and collaborate to successfully develop a system.

Languages, in the broad sense, are not always composed of written words. For example, we commonly use "counting language" to introduce children to counting and arithmetic. A child is given a number of apples, oranges, pebbles, or some other type of object to represent a quantity. For the child, the representation of five might end up being five apples. The operations of addition and subtraction are then represented by the physical action of adding or removing objects from the child's collection. We adults, on the other hand, prefer the language of arithmetic, which represents a specific quantity using a string of Arabic numerals, and which uses the + and - operators to represent addition and subtraction.

Figure 1-2 contrasts a young child's counting language with the more abstract arithmetic language used by adults.

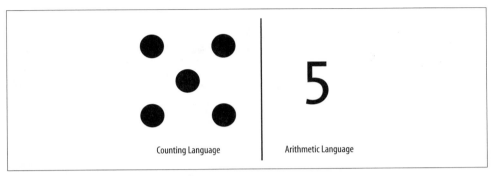

Figure 1-2. The quantity five in two "languages"

Now consider these two languages for communicating some specific number of days for a project. To model and express the quantity of five, the counting language uses five objects while arithmetic uses the string "5". To model and express a more involved quantity of, say, 365, the counting language uses 365 objects (however, having so many objects may be impractical), while the arithmetic language uses the string "365". To model and express the quantity of four and a half, the counting language uses 4 objects and one half of an object (again, however, one half of an object may or may not be practical), and arithmetic uses the string "4.5". Because arithmetic allows us to more easily and practically represent a wider range of quantities than the counting language, arithmetic is said to be more *expressive* than the counting language. Likewise, a quantity is expressed more concisely using arithmetic rather than the counting language. By using languages that are more expressive, we can communicate complex information about complex subjects in a more concise manner than would be possible otherwise.

Stated somewhat formally, the UML is a language for specifying, visualizing, constructing, and documenting the artifacts of a *system-intensive process*. A *system-intensive process* is an approach that focuses on a system, including the steps for producing or maintaining the system given the requirements the system must meet. Specifying involves the creation of a model that describes a system. Visualizing involves the use of diagrams to render and communicate the model (the model is the idea and the diagrams are the expression of the idea). Constructing involves the use of this visual depiction to construct the system, similar to how a blueprint is used to construct a building. Documenting uses models and diagrams to capture our knowledge of the requirements and of the system throughout the process.

The UML itself is not a process. A process applies a set of steps described by a *methodology* to solve a problem and develop a system that satisfies its user's requirements. A *method* addresses only part of the development process; for example, requirements gathering, analysis, design, and so forth, whereas a methodology addresses the whole development process from requirements gathering until the system is made available to its users. The different ways for gathering and using requirements, analyzing requirements, designing a system, and so forth are known as *techniques*. *Artifacts* are work products that are produced and used within a process, including documentation for communication between parties working on a system and the physical system itself. Each type of UML diagram is also known as a *modeling technique*.

Model

A *model* is a representation of a subject. For example, as I noted earlier, to model and express the quantity of five, the counting language uses five objects, whereas arithmetic uses the string "5". A model captures a set of ideas known as *abstractions* about its subject. Without a model, it is very difficult for team members to have a common understanding of the requirements and the system, and for them to consider the impact of changes that occur while the system is being developed.

When creating a model, if we try to represent everything about the subject all at once, we will be easily overwhelmed by the amount of information. Therefore, it is important to focus on capturing relevant information required for understanding the problem at hand, solving that problem, and implementing the solution, while excluding any irrelevant information that may hinder our progress. By managing what abstractions make up a model, how detailed they are, and when to capture them throughout the development process, we can better manage the overall complexity involved in system development.

Unified

The term *unified* refers to the fact that the Object Management Group (OMG), an industry-recognized standardization organization, and Rational Software Corporation created the UML to bring together the information systems and technology industry's best engineering practices. These practices involve applying techniques that allow us to more successfully develop systems. Without a common language, it is difficult for new team members to quickly become productive and contribute to developing a system.

Goals and Scope

By understanding the OMG's goals and scope for the UML, we can better understand the motivations behind the UML. The OMG's goals were to make the UML:

- Ready to use
- Expressive

- Simple
- Precise
- Extensible
- Implementation-independent
- Process-independent

By being ready to use, expressive, simple, and precise, the UML can immediately be applied to development projects. To enable the development of precise models, the OMG introduced the Object Constraint Language (OCL), a sublanguage for attaching conditions that the elements of a model must satisfy for the model to be considered correct (also known as *well formed*). The OCL is discussed in Chapter 10.

An extensible language allows us to define new concepts, similar to introducing new words and extending the vocabulary of a natural language. Extensibility is discussed in Chapter 9. An implementation-independent language may be used independently of any specific implementation technologies, such as Java or .NET. A process-independent language may be used with various types of processes.

The OMG's scope when creating the UML included combining the modeling languages of three of the most prominent system-development methods—Grady Booch's *Booch '93* method, James Rumbaugh's *Object Modeling Technique (OMT) -2* method, and Ivar Jacobson's *Object-Oriented Software Engineering (OOSE)* method—with the information systems and technology industry's best engineering practices. Separately, these are only methods, but together, they form a fairly complete methodology.

History

The UML's history consists of five distinct time periods. By understanding these periods, you can understand why the UML emerged and how it is still evolving today.

The fragmentation period

Between the mid-1970s and the mid-1990s, organizations began to understand the value of software to business but only had a fragmented collection of techniques for producing and maintaining software. Amongst the various emerging techniques and methods that focused on producing and maintaining software more effectively (each having its own modeling languages), three methods stood out:

- Grady Booch's Booch '93 method (from Booch '91) emphasized the design and construction of software systems.
- James Rumbaugh's Object Modeling Technique (OMT) -2 method (from OMT-1) emphasized the analysis of software systems.
- Ivar Jacobson's Object-Oriented Software Engineering (OOSE) method emphasized business engineering and requirements analysis.

As object-oriented methods began to evolve from structured methods, the industry fragmented around these three—and other—methods. Practitioners of one method could not easily understand artifacts produced using a different method. In addition, practitioners encountered problems moving from one organization to the next because such a move frequently entailed learning a new method. Furthermore, tool support was nonexistent to minimal because there were so many methods. Therefore, it was often cost prohibitive to use any method at all.

The unification period

Between the mid-1990s and 1997, the UML 1.0 emerged. James Rumbaugh, and later Ivar Jacobson, joined Grady Booch at Rational Software Corporation to unify their approaches. Because of their unification effort, they became known as the *Three Amigos*. As organizations began to see the value of the UML, the OMG's Object Analysis and Design Task Force issued a Request for Proposal (RFP) to establish a standard that defines the meaning of object-oriented technology concepts for tools that support object-oriented analysis and design. Together with various other organizations, Rational Software Corporation formed the UML Partners Consortium, and the partners submitted Version 1.0 of the UML to the OMG as one of many initial RFP responses.

The standardization period

In the later half of 1997, the UML 1.1 emerged. All the RFP responses were combined into Version 1.1 of the UML. The OMG adopted the UML and assumed responsibility for further development of the standard in November 1997.

The revision period

After adoption of the UML 1.1, various versions of the UML emerged. The OMG charted a revision task force (RTF) to accept public comments on the UML and make minor editorial and technical updates to the standard. Various product and service vendors began to support and promote the UML with tools, consulting, books, and so forth. The current version of the UML is 1.4, and the OMG is currently working on a major revision, UML 2.0.

The industrialization period

In parallel with the revision period, the OMG is proposing the UML standard for international standardization as a Publicly Available Specification (PAS) via the International Organization for Standardization (ISO). The most current version of the UML specification is available from the OMG at *http://www.omg.org*.

The UML and Process

Even though the UML is process-independent, its authors promote a process that is use-case driven, architecture-centric, iterative, and incremental. By understanding how the UML is related to process and the type of process the UML's authors promote, you can better understand how to best approach learning the UML. However, any type of process—even one without these characteristics—may use the UML.

Generally, every system development lifecycle process involves the following types of lifecycle activities:

- Requirements-gathering activities to capture requirements that define what a system should do
- Analysis activities to understand the requirements
- Design activities to determine how a system will satisfy its requirements
- Implementation activities to build a system
- Testing activities to verify that a system satisfies its requirements
- Deployment activities to make a system available to its users

There are many types of approach for applying these activities to develop a system. Traditionally, a waterfall approach has been applied. Now, an iterative approach is more common.

Applying a Waterfall Approach

When applying a *waterfall approach*, lifecycle activities are performed in a single, linear sequence for all the requirements. This often results in the discovery, during testing activities when the different pieces of the system are integrated, of quality-related problems that have remained hidden during the design and implementation activities. Because such problems are discovered late in the development process, it may be too late to resolve them or they may be too costly to resolve. For example, discovering that a specific database management system's performance will be insufficient for the applications that use it after all of the applications have already been developed represents a colossal problem.

Consider a project that involves 10 requirements, perhaps the generation of 10 different types of reports where each report stems from a different requirement. Within a waterfall approach, all the requirements are captured and analyzed, and the whole system is designed, implemented, tested, and deployed in this linear sequence. Within such an approach, the UML may readily be used to communicate the requirements and description of the system. However, because activities are performed in a single linear sequence for all the requirements, the UML models must be fairly complete at each step. This level of completeness is often hard to measure or achieve, because while the UML is more precise than natural languages, it is less precise than programming languages. Therefore, rather than focusing on the system, teams using UML in a waterfall approach often struggle in trying to determine whether their UML models are complete enough.

Applying an Iterative Approach

When applying an *iterative approach*, any subsets of the lifecycle activities are performed several times to better understand the requirements and gradually develop a more robust system. Each cycle through these activities or a subset of these activities is known as an *iteration*, and a series of iterations in a step-wise manner eventually results in the final system. This enables you to better understand the requirements and gradually develop a more appropriate system through successive refinement and incrementally gaining more detail as you do more and more iterations. For example, you can investigate a specific database management system's performance and discover that it will be insufficient for the applications that use it before the applications have been completely developed, and thus make the appropriate modifications to the applications or investigate using another database management system before it becomes too late or too costly.

Consider a project that involves generating 10 different types of reports. Within an iterative approach, the following sequence of iterations is possible:

1. We identify five requirements (named R1 through R5) and analyze three of the five requirements (perhaps R1, R3, and R5).

2. We capture five new requirements (named R6 through R10), analyze the two requirements that were not analyzed in the previous iteration (R2 and R4), and design, implement, and test the system that satisfies the three requirements that were analyzed in the previous iteration (R1, R3, and R5) and the two requirements analyzed in this iteration (R2 and R4), but we don't deploy the system because we did not allocate enough time in the current iteration for that activity.

3. We deploy the system that satisfies the five requirements tested in the previous iteration (R1 through R5) and continue working on the other requirements (R6 through R10).

4. We continue working on the system but must address changes to one requirement that has already been deployed (perhaps R3), changes to other requirements that have not yet been deployed (perhaps R6 and R10), and other technical changes to the system.

This sequence of iterations may appear quite chaotic; however, an iterative approach is only a concept and the UML is only a language; thus, a methodology is required when using the UML on actual projects. When iterations are used by a methodology, they are not chaotic but are organized and quite dynamic within the context of the methodology.

An iterative approach to system development offers the following benefits:

- We can better manage complexity by building a system in smaller increments rather than all at once.

- We can better manage changing requirements by incorporating changes throughout the process and not trying to capture and address all the requirements at once.

- We can provide partial solutions to users throughout the process rather than have them wait until the end of the process, at which time they receive the whole system and perhaps conclude that it is not what they expected.

- We can solicit feedback from users concerning the parts of the system already developed, so we may make changes and guide our progress in providing a more robust system that meets their requirements.

An iterative process is *incremental* because we don't simply rework the same requirements in successive iterations, but address more and more requirements in successive iterations. Likewise, activities may occur in *parallel* within a single iteration when they focus on different parts of the system and don't conflict. Therefore, an iterative approach involves a series of iterations wherein the system is developed incrementally. Even though such an approach is often known as iterative and incremental, it is actually iterative, incremental, and parallel. Because such an approach gradually develops a system through successive refinement and incrementally increasing detail, we are better able to determine the appropriate level of completeness of our UML models than within a waterfall approach. For example, if we have a question or concern that needs to be addressed, and if we are unable to readily use our UML models to address that concern, perhaps we need to elaborate them further; otherwise, we can proceed without spending more time and effort elaborating our UML models.

With such a dynamic approach in which activities within iterations occur in parallel and a system is constructed incrementally, how do we keep our activities organized and driven to satisfy the requirements? How do we maintain focus on the system and avoid constructing a system that may be difficult to maintain and enhance because it is simply a collection of parts glued together without some overarching scheme? What requirements do we address first, and what pieces of the system do we implement first? Answering these questions is where use cases, architecture, and risk management are critical within an iterative approach.

Use cases

A *use case* is a functional requirement described from the perspective of the users of a system. For example, functional requirements for most systems include security functionality allowing users to log in and out of the system, input data, process data, generate reports, and so forth. Use cases are the subject of Chapter 4.

A use-case driven process is one wherein we are able to use use cases to plan and perform iterations. This allows us to organize our activities and focus on implementing the requirements of a system. That is, we capture and analyze use cases, design and implement a system to satisfy them, test and deploy the system, and plan future iterations. Therefore, use cases are the glue between all the activities within an iteration.

Architecture

Architecture encompasses the elements making up a system and the manner in which they work together to provide the functionality of the system. For example, most systems include elements for handling security functionality, inputting and processing data, generating reports, and so forth. The elements and their relationships are known as the system's *structure*. Modeling a system's structure is known as *structural modeling*. Structural modeling is the subject of Part II. The elements and how they interact and collaborate is known as the system's *behavior*. Modeling a system's behavior is known as *behavioral modeling*. Behavioral modeling is the subject of Part III. The different types of elements that constitute a system's architecture, both structure and behavior, are determined by the object-oriented paradigm. The principles and concepts of the object-oriented paradigm are the subject of Chapter 2.

An *architecture-centric* process focuses on the architecture of a system across iterations. This allows us to better ensure that the resulting system is not a hodgepodge of elements that may be difficult to integrate, maintain, and enhance. Therefore, architecture is the glue between all the elements that make up the system as the system is incrementally developed across iterations.

Risk

A *risk* is any obstacle or unknown that may hinder our success. For example, when developing a system, risks include such things as insufficient funding, untrained team members with critical responsibilities, and unstable technologies.

To determine what use cases ought to drive an iteration and what parts of the architecture to focus on in the iteration, we first identify project risks. We then address those use cases that confront the highest risks and those elements of the architecture that, when built, resolve the highest risks. Such an approach is often known as *risk confronting*.

Consider once again the project that involves generating 10 different types of reports. Say that three reports (perhaps R1, R3, and R5) require significant database access, and that four reports (perhaps R3, R6, R8, and R10) require significant user input. Perhaps there are two risks: the risk of not having an intuitive user interface (named X1) and the risk of having an inefficient database management system (named X2). From these descriptions, we know that R1, R3, and R5 are associated with risk X1, and that R3, R6, R8, and R10 are associated with X2. If X1 is more critical to our project, and has a higher possibility of occurring or a higher impact on the project, we would address R1, R3, and R5 or as many of their requirements as possible first, because they confront risk X1. If X2 is more critical to our project, and has a higher possibility of occurring or a higher impact on the project, we would address R3, R6, R8, and R10 or as many of their requirements as possible first because they confront risk X2. However, in either case, we ought to target R3 first, because it addresses both risks.

The UML provides structural and behavioral modeling techniques that may be used in a step-wise process that is driven by requirements, focuses on developing an architecturally sound system that satisfies the requirements, and enables you to confront risks throughout the system-development process.

Learning the UML

Learning the UML can be quite overwhelming given the breadth and depth of the language and its lack of a process if you don't know on what parts of the UML to focus. But by understanding how the UML is related to process, you know to focus on:

- The object-oriented paradigm, because it establishes the foundation for the UML
- Structural modeling and behavioral modeling, because they allow you to understand requirements and architecture
- Other capabilities of the UML

In addition, when learning the UML, it is important to focus on the essentials and understand how to effectively and successfully apply the UML to model systems rather than bog yourself down in trying to learn every comprehensive aspect of the language.

For the remainder of the book, I will use a project management system case study to help you learn how to read, understand, write, and effectively and successfully apply the UML. The objective is not to create a complete or comprehensive model from which to implement the system, but to explore the case study and learn how to effectively and successfully apply the UML to communicate in real-world system development. I've included exercises, so you can practice and improve your skills.

Generally, the project management system in the case study provides functionality to manage projects and resources and to administer the system. It defines the following roles:

Project manager
> Responsible for ensuring a project delivers a quality product within specified time, cost, and resource constraints.

Resource manager
> Responsible for ensuring trained and skilled human resources are available for projects.

Human resource
> Responsible for ensuring that their skills are maintained and that quality work is completed for a project.

System administrator
> Responsible for ensuring that a project management system is available for a project.

More detail about the case study is provided where appropriate throughout the remainder of the book. I purposely don't offer all the detail at once, so that you will see how different information is used with the various UML modeling techniques. That, in turn, will help you know when you should seek such detail, and it's a good illustration of how an iterative approach allows you to steadily gain more detail as a project develops.

Rather than introduce some contrived pseudomethodology or process, I will focus on how to use the various UML diagrams and their elements based upon what each diagram communicates and emphasizes. This will allow us to focus on how the different pieces of the language fit together rather than treat the UML as a hodgepodge of different types of diagrams without any underlying scheme, and you'll be able to more effectively and successfully apply the UML. Chapter 2 focuses on the object-oriented paradigm and how the different pieces of the language fit together. Part II focuses on functional requirements and modeling the structure of the project management system using the UML's structural modeling techniques. Part III focuses on modeling the behavior of the project management system using the UML's behavioral modeling techniques. Part IV introduces some of the other capabilities of the UML, including the OCL and facilities for extending the language.

CHAPTER 2

Object-Oriented Modeling

This chapter introduces the object-oriented paradigm and the UML's modeling techniques. As the UML is a language for communicating about a system and its requirements, we communicate our understanding of the subject using an alphabet, words, sentences, paragraphs, sections, and documents. First, I discuss how to write sentences—UML diagram fragments—about the subject using the language's alphabet and words, and I also introduce the concepts and principles of the object-oriented paradigm. Next, I talk about how sentences are organized into paragraphs—UML diagrams—and I introduce the various UML modeling techniques. Next, I go over how paragraphs are organized into sections—architectural views. Finally, I discuss how sections are organized into documents—models. Many details are not fleshed out in this chapter but are more fully elaborated in subsequent chapters.

Project Management System Requirements

Throughout this chapter, I will use the following partial requirements description of a very small part of the project management system under development as the case study for this book:

> A project manager uses the project management system to manage a project. The project manager leads a team to execute the project within the project's start and end dates. Once a project is created in the project management system, a manager may initiate and later terminate the project due to its completion or for some other reason.

> As input, a project uses requirements. As output, a project produces a system (or part of a system). The requirements and system are work products: things that are created, used, updated, and elaborated throughout a project. Every work product has a description, is of some percent complete throughout the effort, and may be validated. However, validation is dependent on the type of work product. For example, the requirements are validated with users in workshops, and the system is validated by being tested against the requirements. Furthermore, requirements may be published using various types of media, including on an intranet or on paper, and systems may be deployed onto specific platforms.

The project management system must be able to handle the following scenario. Si, who is a manager, manages three projects, named Eagle, Falcon, and Hawk. All projects involve anonymous or unnamed teams. The Eagle project is producing a project management system, similar to the one being described. The Falcon project is using the Java platform to produce another type of system, which is targeted for the broad market. The Hawk project is using the Microsoft .NET platform to produce a system similar to the Falcon project, but one that has additional organization-specific requirements. Therefore, the Falcon and Hawk projects share some common requirements, while the Hawk project has additional organization-specific requirements.

When creating a project, a project manager uses a user interface to enter his contact information (at minimum, a name and phone number), the project's name, the start and end dates, a description of the requirements and the system, and a description of the team. Once the required information is provided, the system appropriately processes the request by storing the information and confirming completion. Initially, the project is inactive. It becomes active when human resources are assigned to the project, may become inactive again if human resources are unassigned from the project, and is removed from the system once it is completed.

For auditing and security purposes, the project management system has two parts, a user interface and database. The database of the project management system executes on a central server. The user interface of the project management system executes on a desktop client computer, has access to a printer, and uses the database to store project-related information.

This description provides significant detail; however, it does not provide all the detail concerning the project management system. By using the UML throughout this chapter, we should be able to better understand this description, and by using a process, we may be able to inquire about missing information to develop the system.

Alphabets, Words, and Sentences

Because requirements and implementation technologies are complex and constantly changing, a language must not only facilitate communication about a subject, but also enable us to better manage change and complexity when we communicate about the subject. A language is based on a *paradigm*, a way of viewing a subject, that defines the types of concepts that may be used in the language and the principles of why they are useful. A language's *syntax* specifies the notation used for communication and is determined by the language's alphabet. A language's *semantics* specify the meaning that is communicated and is determined by the language's words and sentences. The syntax of the UML involves diagrams, and its semantics are based on the object-oriented paradigm.

To communicate using a language, we must understand its alphabet, how its alphabet is used to form words, and how its words are used to form sentences. We must also understand the concepts and principles of its underlying paradigm.

Alphabet

An *alphabet* defines the simplest parts of a language: letters, characters, signs, and marks. For example, the English language has 26 letters. The UML's alphabet consists of symbol fragments (rectangles, lines, and other graphical elements) and strings of characters. These don't have meaning by themselves; the smallest units of meaning in a language are its "words."

Words

A *word* is a grouping of elements from a language's alphabet that defines a unit of meaning. For example, the English language has various words, including "project," "manager," "team," "lead," "execute," and so forth. In the UML, words belong to two broad categories or types:

Concepts
> Concepts are shown as solid-outline rectangles or symbols labeled with a name.

Relationships between concepts
> Relationships between concepts are shown as line paths connecting symbols labeled with a name.

In addition to their names, concepts and relationships may have other strings of characters attached to them specifying other information.

Figure 2-1 shows various concepts identified from the project management system requirements by focusing on nouns, including Project, Manager, Team, Work Product, Requirement, and System.

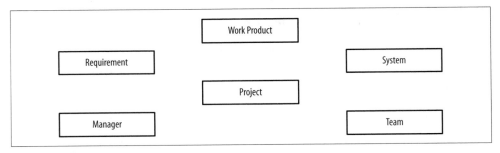

Figure 2-1. Concepts

Likewise, Figure 2-2 shows various relationships identified from the project management system requirements by focusing on verbs, including Manage, Lead, Execute, Input, and Output.

You would not normally show all these relationships in isolation as in Figure 2-2, but would combine them with the concepts shown in Figure 2-1. When you combine relationships with concepts, you are really combining UML words to form UML sentences.

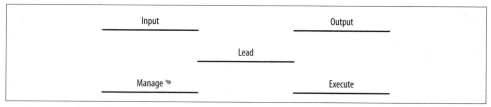

Figure 2-2. Relationships

Sentences

A *sentence* is a grouping of words from a language's vocabulary that defines a grammatical unit of meaning containing a subject and an expression about the subject. A language's *grammar* specifies the rules for combining words to form sentences. For example, the English language has rules for combining words to form sentences, in which the sentence "a manager leads a team" follows the grammar rules, but the sentence "leads manager team" does not. UML sentences are diagram fragments or very simple diagrams.

Figure 2-3 shows a UML sentence communicating that a team will execute a project as indicated in the project management system requirements. Team and Project are concepts (nouns), and Execute is the relationship (verb) between the two concepts.

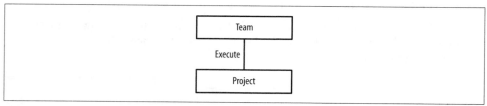

Figure 2-3. A team will execute a project

Figure 2-4 shows a somewhat more elaborate UML sentence in which a manager manages a project and leads a team.

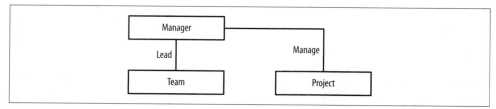

Figure 2-4. A manager manages a project and leads a team (Version 1)

Notice that Figure 2-4 communicates about a manager's relationship with a team and project, but it does not communicate that the team will execute the project, as Figure 2-3 did. Just like the English language, we can communicate whatever we want using the UML. Perhaps one way to look at this is that the UML sentence in Figure 2-4 has a different subject (manager) than the UML sentence in Figure 2-3 (team).

The visual location of concepts and relationships does not have any special meaning so long as symbols are not nested inside one another. A relationship is usually read from left to right and top to bottom; otherwise, its name may have a small black solid triangle arrow next to it where the point of the triangle indicates the direction in which to read the name; the arrow is purely descriptive, and the name of the relationship should be understood by the meaning of the concepts it relates. For example, Figure 2-5 communicates the same information as Figure 2-4.

Figure 2-5. A manager manages a project and leads a team (Version 2)

In Figure 2-5, if I did not show the small black solid triangle arrows next to the relationship, we would still know that managers manage projects and lead teams, because that is what it means to be a manager. This is why it is important to know the semantics of what we depict in the UML rather than simply the syntax. Saying that teams lead managers and projects manage managers would be meaningless!

The Object-Oriented Paradigm

Now that you know how to use simple UML words and sentences, let's consider the object-oriented paradigm on which the UML's semantics are based. We'll look at how object-oriented concepts enable us to view the world around us, and at how the paradigm's principles enable us to better manage change and complexity.

Concepts

The object-oriented paradigm is based on a few key concepts that enable us to view the world around us. The next few sections discuss these key concepts.

Classes, associations, objects, and links

Figures 2-3 through 2-5 represent general sentences, because they don't identify particular projects, managers, teams, and so forth. The general concepts shown in the sentences are known as *classes*, and the general relationships are known as *associations*. Similar to natural languages, we can also communicate in the UML using specific sentences involving specific projects, managers, teams, and so forth, where specific concepts are known as *objects* and specific relationships are known as *links*.

A class defines a type of object and the characteristics of its objects, and an object is an instance of a class. For example, Figures 2-4 and 2-5 show three classes, including Manager, Team, and Project. We can have many managers, teams, and projects, and each specific manager, team, and project is an instance or object of its class. In the UML, a specific concept is shown using the same symbol as its general concept. The symbol is labeled with a specific name followed by a colon followed by the name of its general concept. The entire string—specific name, colon, and general name—is fully underlined. Both names are optional, and the colon is only present if the general concept is specified. Figure 2-6 shows a specific class for each of the three objects shown earlier in Figures 2-4 and 2-5.

An association defines a type of link and the characteristics of its links, and a link is an instance of an association. A specific relationship is shown as a line path and may be labeled with the fully underlined name of its general relationship. Figure 2-6 shows two specific links of the associations shown earlier in Figures 2-4 and 2-5.

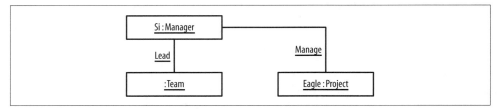

Figure 2-6. Si manages the Eagle project and leads an anonymous team

Figure 2-6, a specific sentence based on the general sentence shown in Figures 2-4 and 2-5, shows that Si, who is a manager, manages the Eagle project and leads an anonymous or unnamed team. This notation and naming convention between a class and its instances, or an association and its instances, is used throughout the UML and is known as a *type-instance dichotomy*.

The object-oriented paradigm views the world as a collection of unique objects, often referred to as a *society of objects*. Each object has a *lifecycle* where it knows something, can do something, and can communicate with other objects. What an object knows and can do are known as *features*. For example, a manager knows his or her name, can initiate or terminate a project, and can communicate with a team to lead the team to successfully execute the project. Features belong to two broad categories or types: attributes and operations.

Attributes

Something that an object knows is called an *attribute*, which essentially represents data. A class defines attributes and an object has values for those attributes. Even if two objects have the same values for their attributes, the objects are unique and have their own identities. In a UML diagram, a class may be shown with a second compartment that lists these attributes as text strings. Likewise, an object may be shown with a second compartment that lists these attributes as text strings, each followed by an equal symbol (=) and its value. Only attributes we wish to communicate are shown; other attributes that are not important for us to communicate on a given diagram need not be shown. Associations and attributes are known as *structural features*, because they communicate the class's structure similar to how structural modeling is used to communicate structure as discussed in Chapter 1.

Figure 2-7 elaborates on Figure 2-4 and shows that a manager has a name, a team has a description, and a project has a name, start date, and end date.

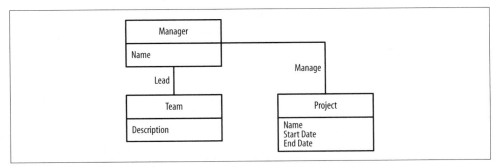

Figure 2-7. Classes with attributes

Figure 2-8 elaborates on Figure 2-6 showing various objects with values for the attributes introduced in Figure 2-7.

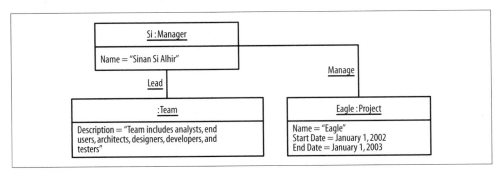

Figure 2-8. Objects with attribute values

Operations and methods

Something an object can do is called an *operation* or *specification* and essentially represents processing. How an object does the processing for a given operation is known as the operation's *method* or *implementation*. For example, when using a programming language, we declare functions or procedures and define their bodies (lines of code) that determine what the functions or procedures do when they are invoked and executed; a function's declaration is the operation, and the body definition is the method. A class defines operations and methods that apply to its objects. A class may be shown with a third compartment that lists these operations as text strings. A class's methods—the code actually implementing the operations—are not shown on a class, but may be described using other UML modeling techniques. An object does not have a third compartment, because all the objects of a class have the same operations and share their class's methods. Likewise, only operations we wish to communicate need be shown on a given diagram. Other operations that are not important for us to communicate on a given diagram need not be shown. If attributes are not shown, an empty attributes compartment must be shown such that the third compartment is used to list the operations. Operations and methods are known as *behavioral features*, because they communicate a class's behavior similar to how behavioral modeling is used to communicate behavior as discussed in Chapter 1.

By showing two operations, `Initiate Project` and `Terminate Project`, Figure 2-9 shows that a manager may initiate or terminate a project. Notice that the second compartment for `Manager` is empty, because I'm focusing only on a manager's operations.

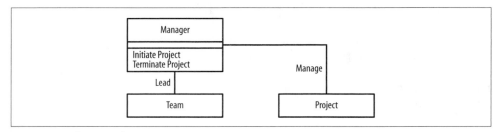

Figure 2-9. Classes with operations

Figure 2-10 combines Figure 2-7 and Figure 2-9 by showing the attributes and operations for each class on the same diagram.

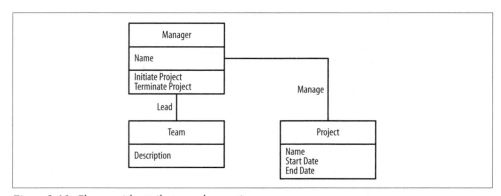

Figure 2-10. Classes with attributes and operations

Messages and stimuli

In the object-oriented paradigm, communication from a sender object to a receiver object is used to convey information or request processing. For example, we don't initiate a project for a manager but communicate a request to the manager to initiate the project. Once the manager receives the request, an operation is invoked to handle the request, and the manager executes the method associated with the operation. The sending of a request and reception of a request are *events*, or occurrences. Communication between objects via their links is called a *stimulus*, and communication between classes via their associations is called a *message*. A stimulus is an instance of a message similar to how an object is an instance of a class and a link is an instance of an association. The sender is known as the *client*, and the receiver is known as the *supplier*. A message or stimulus is shown as an arrow attached to an association or link pointing from the sender toward the receiver and labeled with a sequence number showing the order in which the message or stimulus is sent, followed by a colon followed by the name of the operation to be invoked.

Figure 2-11 shows that a manager assigns activities and tasks to a team based on a project's requirements.

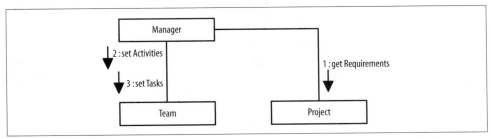

Figure 2-11. General interaction

Figure 2-12 shows a specific interaction between Si (who is a manager), the Eagle project, and the team.

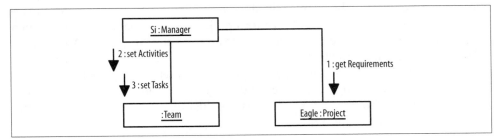

Figure 2-12. Specific interaction

Principles

The object-oriented paradigm is based on four principles that enable us to better manage change and complexity. The next few sections discuss these principles.

Abstractions

Concepts and relationships are known as abstractions. Classes and associations are general abstractions, and objects and links are specific abstractions. A good abstraction is well defined and includes essential information required for understanding it, but excludes any irrelevant or incidental information. For example, when communicating about managers, it is essential that we know their names, but it is not essential for us to know how many pets they own or the types of pets they own, if any. Likewise, by considering various managers, we can determine what similarities and differences they have that allow us to classify them as managers. By using well-defined abstractions, we can better manage complexity by focusing on what is essential rather than being distracted by what is incidental.

Encapsulation

Combining attributes and operations to form classes and objects and hiding methods behind operations is known as *encapsulation*.

Combining attributes and operation to form classes and objects is also known as *localization*. By combining attributes and operations into single units, we can better manage change and complexity by reducing the number of places we have to consider when a change occurs. For example, when there is a change to the Manager class, such as a need to track the manager's years of experience, we simply need to go to the class and update its attributes or operations rather than go to one location to update the manager's data (or attributes) and another location to update its processing (or operations).

When classes or objects communicate, the client is usually interested only in the results of the operation and not the method the supplier uses to perform the operation; thus, a method may be completely hidden from its clients. For example, a manger is interested in having the team execute a project, but the manger is not so much interested in the intricate details of how the team executes the project. An attribute may also be made inaccessible or hidden from clients in that it must be accessed via operations, called *getters* and *setters*, which retrieve and set the value of the attribute. For instance, how the budget associated with a project is stored may be hidden from clients, in that it is either stored in a database or a flat file, and is accessible via getter and setter operations.

Hiding a method behind an operation is also known as *information hiding*. Doing this allows us to better manage change and complexity, because we are able to modify a class's method without impacting its clients who use the operation implemented by the method. For example, when a manager directs the team to execute a project, the team may use various techniques, and may change techniques without impacting the manager. Also, the getters and setters for the budget associated with a project may be changed to store the budget in a database instead of a flat file, or vice versa, without impacting clients.

Generalization

Figure 2-13 shows the classes that represent requirements and systems based on the requirements for the project management system case study. Note that requirements and systems are work products with some similar attributes and operation but different methods for validation and various attributes unique to their classes. That is, both systems and requirements have a Percent Complete attribute and a Description attribute, but requirements also have a Media attribute while systems have a Platform attribute. While both systems and requirements have a Validate operation, requirements also have a Publish operation while systems have a Deploy operation. We can use a generalization to capture and reuse their commonality. A *generalization* is used between a more general class and a more specific class to indicate that the more specific class receives the attributes, relationships, operations, and methods from the more general class. A generalization is shown as a solid-line path from the more specific class to the more general class, with a large hollow triangle at the end of the path connected to the more general class.

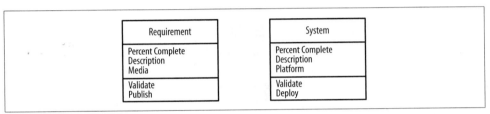

Figure 2-13. Project requirements and systems

Figure 2-14 shows how a generalization is used to communicate that both requirements and systems are work products that have a description, percent complete, and may be validated. Notice that the Validate operation has been moved into the Work Product class, similar to the Description and Platform attributes, but the Validate operation also appears in the Requirement class and System classes. In the next section, I will discuss why the Validate operation appears in all the classes. By using a generalization, we can better manage change and complexity. We gain the ability to reuse existing abstractions to define new abstractions, and changes we make to a more general class are propagated to its more specific classes. For example, we can use the Work Product class to define other types of work products such as user documentation, installation and administration manuals, and so forth as necessary in the future.

Polymorphism

Figure 2-14 shows that the Validate operation appears in all the classes. It is identified or declared in the Work Product class, perhaps with a default method, but the Requirement class and System class provide their own methods for validation. Hence the need for the Requirement and System classes to list their own Validate operations.

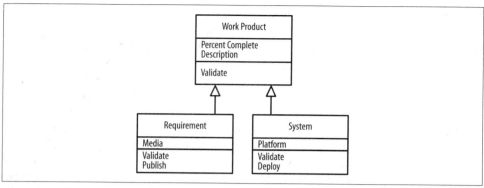

Figure 2-14. Project work products, requirements, and systems

Had these classes simply inherited the default `Validate` functionality from the `Work Product` class, you wouldn't list the `Validate` method again. The ability to have multiple methods for a single operation is called *polymorphism*.

Because a generalization between a more general class and a more specific class also indicates that objects of the more specific class are simply specialized objects of the general class, objects of the specific class may be substituted for objects of the general class. For example, requirements and systems may be substituted for work products. Simply applying the `Validate` operation on a work product without knowing its actual class causes the appropriate method to be invoked. By using polymorphism, we can better manage change and complexity by reusing operations with new methods, and we can communicate requests without having to manage which actual methods are invoked. That is, we can manipulate requirement work products, system work products, and other specific types of work products simply as general types of work products. For every requirement work product, the `Validate` method provided by the `Requirement` class is invoked to handle validation requests. For every system work product, the `Validate` method provided by the `System` class is invoked to handle validation requests, and so forth for any other types of work products.

Paragraphs

A paragraph is a grouping of sentences about a common subject. For example, the English language groups sentences into paragraphs, such as the one you are currently reading. UML paragraphs are diagrams. A *diagram* is a collection of UML sentences. The elements that make up a diagram are known as *diagram elements*. For example, all the elements on the figures shown earlier are diagram elements.

The main subject about which we communicate is a system that resides in a domain. A *domain*, also known as a *context*, is a broad area of interest that has a generally accepted collection of concepts and their relationships. These concepts are classes, and their relationships are associations; both are known as *domain elements*. For example, the project management system may be used to manage projects in various industries, including product manufacturing, strategic services, financial services, information technology consulting, and so forth, and each industry is a different domain. Understanding a user's domain is critical as a launching point for developing a system that the user and other *stakeholders* (those having a stake or interest in the project) will find useful and valuable.

A *system* is a collection of elements organized together for a specific purpose. These elements are known as *system elements*. To understand a system, we focus on its architecture. The architecture of a system involves the elements that make up the system and the way they work together to provide the functionality of the system. The major elements that make up a system are known as *architectural elements*. A system's elements and their relationships define the system's structure, and the way the elements interact and collaborate define the system's behavior.

A system may be recursively decomposed into smaller systems, called *subsystems* and *primitive elements*. Subsystems may be further decomposed into *sub-subsystems* and primitive elements, and so forth. When fully decomposed, a system and all its subsystems consist of primitive elements. Primitive elements cannot be further decomposed. For example, the project management system can be decomposed into the following:

- A user interface subsystem responsible for providing an interface through which users can interact with the system.
- A business processing subsystem responsible for implementing business functionality.
- A data subsystem responsible for implementing data storage functionality.

When the primitive elements of a system or subsystem are objects, the system is considered an *object-oriented system*. When the primitive elements are simply data elements and functions or procedures, the system is considered a *non-object-oriented system*.

The UML provides various modeling techniques for communicating using diagrams. Each type of diagram emphasizes something about a system, and any number of diagrams may be used to communicate about a system. The next sections introduce these diagram types using the project management system requirements provided at the beginning of this chapter. Each diagram is further explored in Parts II and III of this book.

In addition to the diagram types shown in the following sections, the UML allows us to define our own diagrams, as necessary. For example, we can define a database schema diagram that communicates the tables in a database and their relationships. In the UML, diagrams belong to two broad categories or types: structural and behavioral. Also, there are other, more general elements that apply to both types of diagrams.

Structural Modeling

Structural modeling assists in understanding and communicating the elements that make up a system and the functionality the system provides. The following sections briefly introduce the various structural modeling diagrams provided by the UML. Part II describes each diagram type in more detail.

Class diagrams

Class diagrams depict the structure of a system in general. Class diagrams have the following types of elements:

A class
> Shown as a solid-outline rectangle labeled with a name, this represents a general concept.

An association
> Shown as a solid-line path labeled with a name, this represents a relationship between classes.

An attribute
> Shown as a text string in a class's second compartment, this represents what objects of the class know.

An operation
> Shown as a text string in a class's third compartment, this represents what objects of the class can do.

Figure 2-15 is based on the following paragraphs from the requirements description provided at the beginning of the chapter, and combines many of the sentences discussed in the figures shown earlier in this chapter:

> A project manager uses the project management system to manage a project. The project manager leads a team to execute the project within the project's start and end dates. Once a project is created in the project management system, a manager may initiate and later terminate the project due to its completion or for some other reason.

> As input, a project uses requirements. As output, a project produces a system (or part of a system). The requirements and system are work products: things that are created, used, updated, and elaborated on throughout a project. Every work product has a description, is of some percent complete throughout the effort, and may be validated. However, validation is dependent on the type of work product. For example, the requirements are validated with users in workshops, and the system is validated by being tested against the requirements. Furthermore, requirements may be published using various types of media, including on an intranet or in paper form; and systems may be deployed onto specific platforms.

These paragraphs describe some of the classes that make up the project management system. We can communicate this information on a single diagram as shown in Figure 2-15, or by using multiple diagrams, as done throughout the earlier part of this chapter. Chapter 3 describes class diagrams in detail.

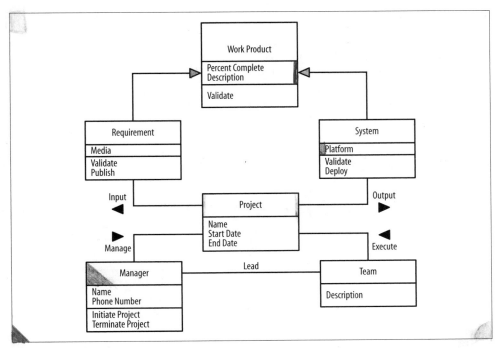

Figure 2-15. Class diagram

Object diagrams

Object diagrams depict the structure of a system at a particular point in time. Object diagrams have the following types of elements:

An object
> Shown as a solid-outline rectangle labeled with a name followed by a colon followed by the name of its class, all fully underlined, this represents a specific concept. Both names are optional, and the colon is only present if the class is specified.

A link
> Shown as a solid-line path labeled with the name of its association fully underlined, this represents a specific relationship between objects.

An attribute value
> Shown as a text string followed by an equal symbol and its value in an object's second compartment, this represents what the object knows.

Figure 2-16 is based on the following paragraph from the requirements description provided at the beginning of the chapter:

> The project management system must be able to handle the following scenario. Si, who is a manager, manages three projects, named Eagle, Falcon, and Hawk. All projects involve anonymous or unnamed teams. The Eagle project is producing a

project management system, similar to the one being described. The Falcon project is using the Java platform to produce another type of system, which is targeted for the broad market. The Hawk project is using the Microsoft .NET platform to produce a system similar to the Falcon project, but one that has additional organization-specific requirements. Therefore, the Falcon and Hawk projects share some common requirements, while the Hawk project has additional organization-specific requirements.

This paragraph describes a specific situation that the project management system must be able to handle using the various classes that make up the system. We can communicate this information on a single diagram, as shown in Figure 2-16, or by using multiple diagrams, as has been done earlier in this chapter. Chapter 3 describes object diagrams in detail.

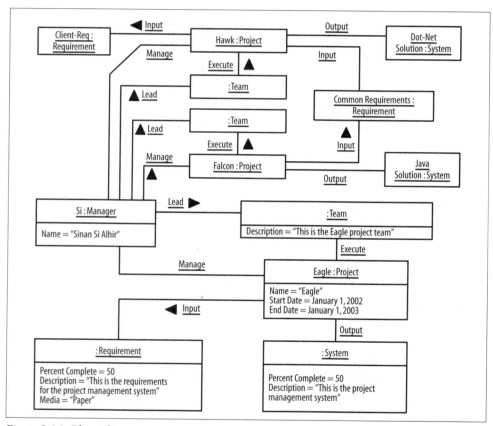

Figure 2-16. Object diagram

Use-case diagrams

Use-case diagrams depict the functionality of a system. Use-case diagrams have the following types of elements:

An actor
> Shown as a "stick figure" icon, this represents users and external systems with which the system we are discussing interacts.

A use case
> Shown as an ellipse, this represents a functional requirement that is described from the perspective of the users of a system.

A communicate association
> Shown as a solid-line path from an actor to a use case, this represents that the actor uses the use case.

Figure 2-17 is based on the following part of a paragraph from the requirements description provided at the beginning of the chapter:

> A project manager uses the project management system to manage a project.

This identifies specific functionality that the project management system must provide to its users. Chapter 4 describes use-case diagrams in detail.

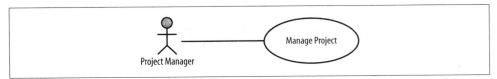

Figure 2-17. Use-case diagram

Component diagrams

Component diagrams, also known as *implementation diagrams*, depict the implementation of a system. Component diagrams have the following types of elements:

A component
> Shown as a rectangle with two small rectangles protruding from its side, this represents a part of the system that exists while the system is executing.

A dependency relationship
> Shown as a dashed arrow from a client component to a suppler component, this represents that the client component uses or depends on the supplier component.

Figure 2-18 is based on the following part of a paragraph from the requirements description provided at the beginning of the chapter:

> For auditing and security purposes, the project management system has two parts, a user interface and database.

This paragraph describes how the project management system is implemented when it is executing. Chapter 5 describes component diagrams in detail.

While the object-oriented paradigm focuses on using objects, the *component-based paradigm* focuses on using components. Both paradigms are based on the principles of abstraction, encapsulation, generalization, and polymorphism.

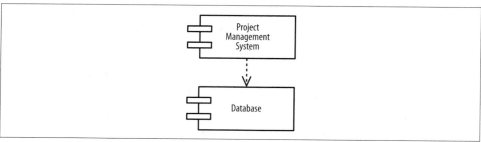

Figure 2-18. Component diagram

Deployment diagrams

Deployment diagrams, also known as *implementation diagrams*, depict the implementation environment of a system. Note that both component and deployment diagrams are specific types of implementation diagrams. Deployment diagrams have the following types of elements:

A node
> Shown as a three-dimensional rectangle, this represents a resource that is available during execution time. A component that resides on a node is nested inside the node.

A communication association
> Shown as a solid-line path between nodes, this represents a communication path between the nodes.

Figure 2-19 is based on the following part of a paragraph from the requirements description provided at the beginning of the chapter:

> The database of the project management system executes on a central server. The user interface of the project management system executes on a desktop client computer, has access to a printer, and uses the database to store project-related information.

This describes the implementation environment of the project management system. Chapter 5 describes deployment diagrams in detail.

Behavioral Modeling

Behavioral modeling assists in understanding and communicating how elements interact and collaborate to provide the functionality of a system. The UML supports a number of diagrams useful for behavioral modeling, and these are briefly described in the following sections. Part III describes these types of diagrams in more detail.

Sequence diagrams

Sequence diagrams, also known as *interaction diagrams*, depict how elements interact over time. A horizontal axis shows the elements involved in the interaction, and a

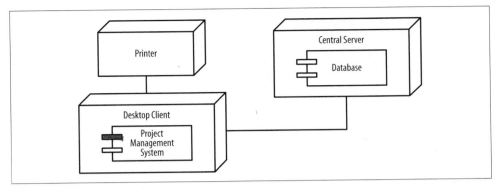

Figure 2-19. Deployment diagram

vertical axis represents time proceeding down the page. Sequence diagrams have the following types of elements:

Classes and objects
 Classes are shown much the same way as on class diagrams. Objects may also be shown much the same way as on object diagrams. In Chapter 6, you will encounter *roles,* which define placeholders for classes and objects.

A lifeline
 Shown as a vertical dashed line from an element, this represents the existence of the element over time.

A communication
 Shown as a horizontal solid arrow from the lifeline of the sender to the lifeline of the receiver and labeled with the name of the operation to be invoked, this represents that the sender sends a message or stimulus to the receiver.

Figure 2-20 is based on the following part of a paragraph from the requirements description provided at the beginning of the chapter:

> When creating a project, a project managers use a user interface to enter their contact information (at minimum, a name and phone number), the project's name, start and end dates, a description of the requirements and system, and a description of the team. Once the required information is provided, the system processes the request appropriately by storing the information and confirming completion.

This paragraph describes a specific scenario the classes and objects that make up the project management system must be able to handle. Chapter 6 describes sequence diagrams in detail.

Collaboration diagrams

Collaboration diagrams, also known as *interaction diagrams,* depict how elements interact over time and how they are related. Note that both sequence and collaboration diagrams are specific types of interaction diagrams. Collaboration diagrams have the types of elements that are described in the list shown next.

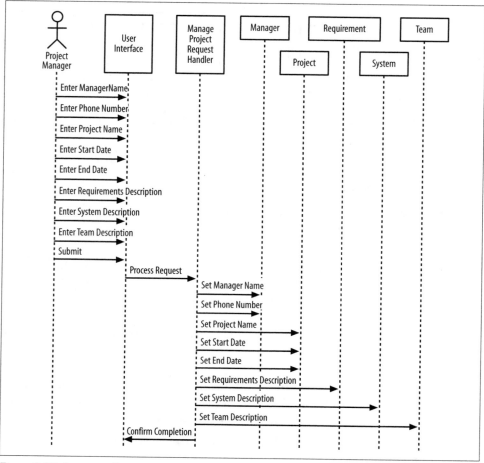

Figure 2-20. Sequence diagram

Classes and objects

Classes are shown much the same way as on class diagrams. Objects may also be shown much the same way as on object diagrams. Again, in Chapter 6, you will encounter roles that define placeholders for classes and objects.

Associations

These are shown much the same way as on class diagrams. Links may also be shown much the same way as on object diagrams.

A communication

This is shown as an arrow attached to a relationship pointing from the sender toward the receiver. It is labeled with a sequence number showing the order in which the communication is sent followed by a colon followed by the name of the operation to be invoked. It represents that the sender sends a message to the receiver.

Figure 2-21 is based on the same part from the requirements description provided at the beginning of the chapter as Figure 2-20 but additionally includes the relationships. Chapter 6 describes collaboration diagrams in detail.

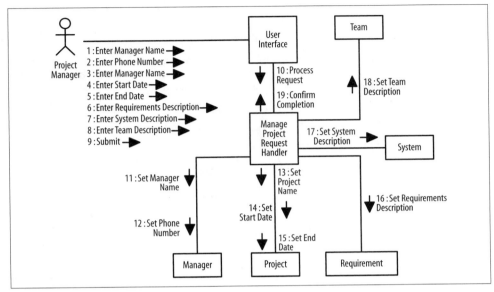

Figure 2-21. Sequence diagram

State diagrams

State diagrams, also known as *statechart diagrams*, depict the lifecycle of an element. State diagrams have the following types of elements:

A state
Shown as a rectangle with rounded corners, this represents a condition or situation of an element.

An event
This is an occurrence of receiving a message.

A transition
Shown as a solid line from a source state to a target state labeled with an event, this represents that if the element is in the source state and the event occurs, it will enter the target state.

Initial state
When an element is created, it enters its *initial state*, which is shown as a small, solid, filled circle. The transition originating from the initial state may be labeled with the event that creates the element.

Final state

When an element enters its *final state*, which is shown as a circle surrounding a small solid filled circle (a bull's eye), it is destroyed. The transition to the final state may be labeled with the event that destroys the element.

Figure 2-22 is based on the following part of a paragraph from the requirements description provided at the beginning of the chapter:

> Initially, the project is inactive. It becomes active when human resources are assigned to the project, may become inactive again if human resources are unassigned from the project, and is removed from the system once it is completed.

This paragraph describes the lifecycle of a project object that makes up the project management system. Chapter 7 describes state diagrams in detail.

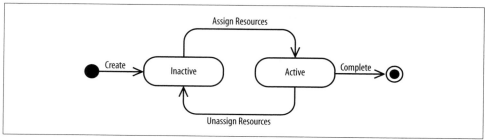

Figure 2-22. Sequence diagram

Activity diagrams

Activity diagrams depict the activities and responsibilities of elements. Activity diagrams have the following types of elements:

An action state

Shown as a shape with straight top and bottom with convex arcs on the two sides, this represents processing.

A control-flow transition

Shown as a solid line from a source action state to a target action state, this represents that once the source action state completes its processing, the target action state starts its processing.

An initial action state

Shown as a small solid filled circle, the control-flow transition originating from the initial state specifies the first action state.

A final action state

Shown as a circle surrounding a small solid filled circle (a bull's eye), the control-flow transition to the final state specifies the final action state.

An object-flow

Shown as a dashed arrow between an action state and an object, this represents that the action state inputs or outputs the object. An input object flow, which points to an action state, represents that the action state inputs the object. An output object flow, which points to an object, represents that the action state outputs the object.

A swimlane

Shown as a visual region separated from neighboring swimlanes by vertical solid lines on both sides and labeled at the top with the element responsible for action states within the swimlane, this represents responsibility.

Figure 2-23 is based on the same part of the requirements description provided at the beginning of the chapter as Figures 2-20 and 2-21, but emphasizes the activities and responsibilities of a project manager and the project management system. Chapter 8 describes activity diagrams in detail.

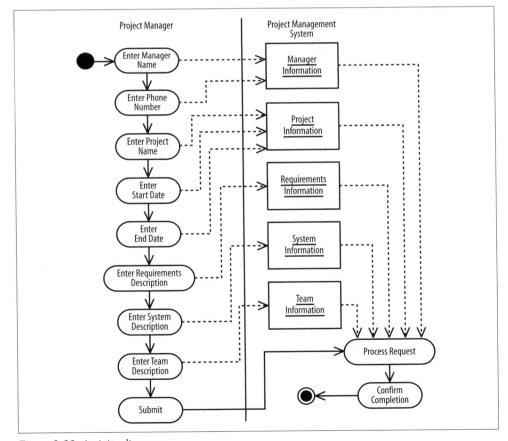

Figure 2-23. Activity diagram

Other Elements

A language often contains elements that are purely notational and other elements that allow for extending the language. UML is no different. UML provides notational items such as notes. Stereotypes and properties allow you to extend the UML.

Notes

A *note*, shown as a rectangle with a bent upper-right corner that may be attached to another element using a dashed line, represents a comment similar to comments in programming languages.

Figure 2-24 shows a comment attached to the Project class.

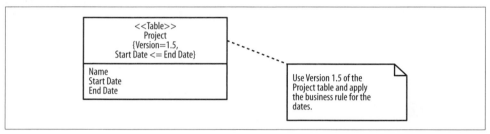

Figure 2-24. Notes, stereotypes, and properties

Stereotypes

A *stereotype*, shown as a text string keyword enclosed in guillemets («», pronounced gee-a-may) or double-angle brackets, before or above the name of an element, represents a specific meaning associated with the element.

Figure 2-24 shows a stereotype attached to the Project class in this example, indicating that the class represents a database table. Chapter 9 describes stereotypes in more detail.

Properties

Properties are shown as a comma-delimited list of text strings inside a pair of braces ({}) after or below the name of an element, and expressed in any natural or computer language, represents characteristics of the element. The text string representing a property can take on two forms:

- A text string may be a *tagged value*, shown as a keyword-value pair (a keyword followed by an equal sign followed by its value) that represents a characteristic of the element and its value.
- A text string may be a *constraint*, shown as a text string that may be expressed in the Object Constraint Language (OCL) that represents a condition the element must satisfy.

Figure 2-24 shows the properties of the Project class, including the version that is used, as well as the business rule concerning the start and end dates of a project. Chapter 9 describes properties in more detail, and Chapter 10 describes the OCL in more detail.

Sections

A UML section is a grouping of paragraphs about a common subject. For instance, the English language groups paragraphs into sections, such as the one you are currently reading. UML sections are architectural views. An *architectural view* is a category of diagrams addressing a specific set of concerns. All the different architectural views determine the different ways in which we can understand a system. For example, all the figures shown so far in this chapter may be organized into different views, including those for addressing functional, structural, behavioral, and other pieces of the project management system. The elements that make up a view are known as *view elements*. For example, all the elements in the figures are view elements when we classify the diagram on which they appear into a specific view.

Because the UML is a language and not a methodology, it does not prescribe any explicit architectural views, but the UML diagrams may be generally organized around the following commonly used architectural views:

The use-case or user architectural view
> Focuses on the functionality of a system, using use-case diagrams to communicate what functionality the system provides to its users.

The structural or static architectural view
> Focuses on the structure of a system, using class and object diagrams to communicate what elements and relationships make up the system.

The behavioral or dynamic architectural view
> Focuses on the behavior of a system, using sequence, collaboration, state, and activity diagrams to communicate the interactions and collaborations of the elements that make up the system.

The component or implementation architectural view
> Focuses on the implementation of a system, using component diagrams to communicate how the system is implemented.

The deployment or environment model architectural view
> Focuses on the implementation environment, using deployment diagrams to communicate how the implemented system resides in its environment.

Even though each type of diagram is organized around a single architectural view, any diagram type can be used in any architectural view. For example, an interaction diagram can be used in a use-case view to communicate how users interact with a system. Furthermore, the UML allows us to define our own architectural views, as necessary. For example, we can define a data store architectural view, and we can define a new type of diagram, perhaps called a database schema diagram, to communicate the tables in a database and their relationships. We could then use other types of diagrams to communicate the triggers and stored procedures in a database.

Documents

A UML document is a grouping of sections about a common subject, including any non-UML diagrams, textual documents, and other supporting information. UML documents are models. For example, the English language groups sections into documents, such as this book. A *model* is a representation of a system. For example, all the figures in this chapter and their supporting textual documentation are a model of the project management system. The elements that make up a model are known as *model elements*. For example, any element used on the diagrams in this chapter, with any supporting documentation necessary for communicating about that element, forms a model element.

The relationship between models, architectural views, and diagrams is similar to the relationship between databases, views, and queries. A database houses data, views organize subsets of the data into meaningful information, and queries extract subsets of the information. A model element is similar to a data element in the database, view elements are similar to data elements used within views, and diagram elements are similar to data elements used within queries. This establishes a general scheme or approach for how the UML is organized and how it allows us to communicate.

Because the UML is a language and not a methodology, it does not prescribe any explicit steps for applying models to develop a system given its requirements, but any methodology may generally address the models in association with these architectural views.

Models and diagrams help us capture and communicate our understanding of the requirements and system throughout the system development lifecycle process. They not only enable us to manage change and complexity, but also to assess our understanding before spending resources in producing a system that is unacceptable or does not sufficiently satisfy the requirements. Models capture all the detail in crossing the chasm between requirements and systems; we surely don't capture design and implementation details in the requirements, and we surely don't capture detailed requirements in the implementation of the system. However, we capture such details in a model that matures throughout a process as our understanding of the requirements and system likewise mature.

Structural Modeling

CHAPTER 3

Class and Object Diagrams

This chapter focuses on class and object diagrams, which depict the structure of a system in general and at a particular point in time, respectively. First, I introduce class and object diagrams and how they are used. Next, I discuss classes, objects, and their details for modeling the elements that make up a system. Then, I go over associations, links, and their details for modeling the relationships among the elements that make up a system. Finally, I discuss various other types of elements and relationships. Many details that were not fleshed out in Chapter 2 are more fully elaborated here, and throughout the chapter I include suggestions relating to class and object diagrams.

Class modeling is a specialized type of modeling concerned with the general structure of a system. Object modeling is a specialized type of modeling concerned with the structure of a system at a particular point in time. You usually apply class and object modeling during analysis and design activities to understand the requirements and determine how a system will satisfy its requirements. Object modeling is usually used in conjunction with class modeling to explore and refine class diagrams. Class and object modeling usually start after the requirements have matured enough (as determined by your system development process) and continue in parallel with interaction and collaboration modeling (Chapter 6) throughout the system development process, while focusing on the elements that make up the system and their relationships.

As an architecture-centric process focuses on the architecture of a system across iterations, it is important to understand what elements make up a system and how they are related to one another. Given that every project has limited resources, you can use this information to determine how best to develop a system. This allows architects, designers, and developers to consider technical trade-offs concerning the system, including which elements can be developed in parallel, which elements can be purchased rather than built, and which elements can be reused.

Classes and Objects

Class diagrams show classes that represent concepts, while object diagrams show objects that represent specific instances of those concepts. The next few sections talk in detail about the representation of classes and objects in class and object diagrams.

Classes

As discussed in Chapter 2, a *class* is a general concept. For example, the project management system involves various general concepts, including projects, managers, teams, work products, requirements, and systems.

A class defines a type of object and its characteristics, including structural features and behavioral features. *Structural features* define what objects of the class know, and *behavioral features* define what objects of the class can do. For example, in Chapter 2 you saw that individuals of the Manager class have names (something they know), and can initiate and terminate projects (things they do). Structural features include attributes and associations. Behavioral features include operations and methods.

The most crucial aspect of a class is that it has semantics: some agreed upon meaning between whomever is communicating about it. For example, when I discuss a project, what does a project mean to my audience? Is it an effort that lasts one week or one year? Is it an effort that requires a manager and other human resources? And so forth. Such meaning is very specific to the audience and domain in which the class is used.

In a UML class diagram, a class is shown as a solid-outline rectangle with three standard compartments separated by horizontal lines. The required top compartment shows the class name, the optional second compartment shows a list of attributes, and the optional third compartment shows a list of operations. The second and third compartments need only show the specific information you want to communicate using a given diagram. You don't need to show all of a class's attributes and operations all the time.

Figure 3-1 shows various fundamental classes associated with the project management system in our case study, including Worker, UnitOfWork, and WorkProduct, using the most basic notation for classes.

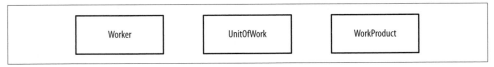

Figure 3-1. Classes

A worker is a person or group of people who perform work, including project managers, resource managers, human resources, and system administrators. A unit of work is a unit of effort, which includes capturing and analyzing requirements, as well as designing, implementing, testing, or deploying a system. A work product is anything produced and used within a project, including the requirements and the system. Notice that a class should be named using a noun phrase. Classes, as you should recall from Chapter 2, represent concepts that you discover by focusing on nouns.

Attributes

An *attribute* is what an object of a class knows. It's an element of data maintained by the object. For example, each object of the Worker class of the project management system may have a name, description, and so forth. These are all attributes.

In a class diagram, you list attributes in the second compartment for a class. The simplest approach is to just list attribute names, but the UML allows you to do much more than that. Consider an attribute for holding a worker's email address. You may start by defining it using the following basic syntax:

```
EmailAddress
```

As you go through the development process, you can add detail to this definition in each iteration by asking various questions and capturing more detail about the attribute based upon the answers.

For example, you may ask how many email addresses a worker has. Presuming that a worker may have up to five email addresses, you can update the attribute definition to the following:

```
EmailAddress [1..5]
```

Next, you may ask if these email addresses are ordered, perhaps by priority. Presuming that email addresses are not ordered, you can update the attribute definition as follows:

```
EmailAddress [1..5 unordered]
```

You may decide to ask the type of data an email address attribute needs to hold. You discover that an email address is a string of characters, and you update the attribute definition to indicate that:

```
EmailAddress [1..5 unordered] : String
```

You might then ask if there should be a default value for a worker's email address. Your client suggests using a default value of "No email address", so you update the attribute definition to the following:

```
EmailAddress [1..5 unordered] : String = "No email address"
```

Finally, you may ask whether other objects are allowed to access a Worker object's email address. Presuming the answer is that a Worker object's email address is not accessible by other objects, you can update the attribute definition one last time by preceding it with minus sign (-), as follows:

```
- EmailAddress [1..5 unordered] : String = "No email address"
```

To summarize, this final attribute definition communicates the following information:

The - symbol
> Indicates that the email address attribute is private to an object and thus inaccessible by other objects.

`1..5`
> Indicates that the email address attribute may have from one to five values.

`unordered`
> Indicates that the email address attribute values are not ordered based on any specific criteria.

`String`
> Indicates that email addresses are strings of characters.

`"No email address"`
> Is the initial value of each email address.

Figure 3-2 shows the `Worker` class from Figure 3-1 with its attributes. A worker has an identification number (`ID`), a next identification number (`NextID`), a name, up to five email addresses that are unordered, any number of phone numbers that are ordered, and a password. `NextID` is underlined to indicate that it is one value, defined at the class level, shared by all objects of the class. The system uses this shared value to ensure that every `Worker` object has a unique ID number.

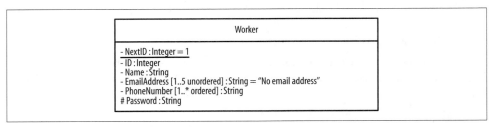

Figure 3-2. Worker class with its attributes

In Figure 3-2, you'll see some syntax I haven't described yet: a number sign (#) at the front of the `Password` attribute and the keyword `ordered` in the `PhoneNumber` attribute. This syntax is described in the next section, "Attribute syntax."

Figure 3-3 shows the `UnitOfWork` class of Figure 3-1 with its attributes. A unit of work has a name and description.

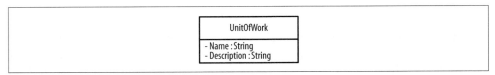

Figure 3-3. UnitOfWork class with its attributes

Figure 3-4 shows the WorkProduct class of Figure 3-1 with its attributes. A work product has a name, description, and a percentage of completion.

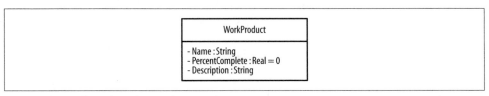

Figure 3-4. WorkProduct class with its attributes

Attribute syntax

In the UML, an attribute is described in a class's second compartment expressed using the following UML syntax:

```
visibility name [multiplicity ordering] : type = initial_value
```

in which:

visibility

Is optional, has no default value, and indicates whether the attribute is accessible from outside the class. It may be one of the following:

+ Public visibility; the attribute is accessible from outside its class.

- Private visibility; the attribute is inaccessible from outside its class.

Protected visibility; the attribute is accessible by classes that have a generalization relationship (as discussed in Chapter 2) to its class, but is otherwise inaccessible from outside its class.

Figures 3-2 through 3-4 show that most attributes are private, except a worker's password is protected so that more specific types of workers may use it in whatever manner in which they handle security.

name

Is the name of the attribute you are describing.

multiplicity

Is optional, has a default value of 1, and indicates the number of values an attribute may hold. If an attribute has only one value, the multiplicity, ordering, and square brackets are not shown. Otherwise, the multiplicity is shown as a lower-bound `..` upper-bound string in which a single asterisk indicates an unlimited range; for example, 0..* allows from zero up to an infinite number of values. Figures 3-2 through 3-4 show that all attributes except for EmailAddress and PhoneNumber have one value only. A worker may have up to five email addresses and any number of phone numbers.

ordering

>Is optional, has a default value of unordered, and is used where the multiplicity is greater than one to indicate whether the values of an attribute are ordered or unordered. Use one of the following keywords:

>unordered

>>Indicates that the values are unordered.

>ordered

>>Indicates that the values are ordered.

>Figure 3-2 shows that a worker's five email addresses are unordered and that a worker's phone numbers are ordered.

type

>Is optional, has no default value, and indicates the type of data an attribute may hold. If you don't show a type for an attribute, you should omit the colon. The type of an attribute may be another class. In addition, the UML provides the following data types:

>Boolean

>>A true or false value

>Integer

>>An integer number

>Real

>>A real number

>String

>>A sequence of characters

>Figures 3-2 through 3-4 show that most of the attributes are strings while a worker's identification number (ID) and next identification number (NextID) are integers, and a work product's PercentComplete attribute is a real number.

initial_value

>Is optional, and indicates the initial value of an attribute. By default, an attribute has no initial value. If you do not show an initial value, you should omit the equal symbol (=). Figures 3-2 through 3-4 show that most of the attributes have no initial value. However, a worker's next identification number (NextID) has an initial value of 1, a work product's percent complete has an initial value of 0, and email addresses have an initial value of "No email address".

If you prefer, the UML also allows you to show an attribute using pseudocode or another language. For example, you can use the syntax of Java, C++, C#, or some other programming language.

If an attribute's value is specific to an object, it is known as *instance scoped* or *object scoped*. If an attribute is shared by all objects of a class, it is known as *class scoped*. To indicate that an attribute is class scoped, underline it. Figures 3-2 through 3-4 show that all the attributes are object scoped, except for the worker's next identification number (NextID), which is class scoped.

Operations

Recall from Chapter 2 that an operation is what an object of a class can do. It is a specification of a service provided by the object. Recall also that a method is how an object of a class does its processing. It is an implementation of a service provided by the object. For example, each class of the project management system may provide getter and setter operations for its attributes. These getter and setter operations retrieve and set the values for the attributes of a worker, unit of work, work product, and so forth.

Consider an operation for adding an email address to a worker. You may start by defining it using the following basic syntax:

```
addEmailAddress
```

As you go through iterations of the development process, you can add detail to this definition by asking questions and capturing additional detail about the operation from the answers to those questions.

For example, you may ask if the `addEmailaddress` operation requires any parameters: data that is input to or output from the operation. Presuming that the operation requires an email address as input, you can update the operation definition to the following:

```
addEmailAddress (theEmailAddress)
```

Next, you may ask what type of data may the email address hold? Presuming that the email address is a string of characters, you can update the operation definition to the following:

```
addEmailAddress (theEmailAddress : String)
```

Next, you may ask if there is a default value for the email address. Presuming that the email address has a default value of an empty string, or no characters, you can update the operation definition to the following:

```
addEmailAddress (theEmailAddress : String = "")
```

You might then ask whether the email address is simply an input to the operation, an output from the operation, or both. Presuming that the email address is only input to the operation, and thus not modified by the operation, you can add the `in` keyword preceding the parameter name:

```
addEmailAddress (in theEmailAddress : String = "")
```

You may then ask whether the operation returns any type of data. Presuming that the operation returns a Boolean true or false indicating whether the operation was successful in adding the email address to the worker, you can update the operation definition to the following:

```
addEmailAddress (in theEmailAddress : String = "") : Boolean
```

Finally, you may ask whether other objects are allowed to access an object's `addEmailAddress` operation. Presuming that an object's `addEmailAddress` operation is accessible by other objects, you can precede the operation name in the definition with a plus sign (+):

```
+ addEmailAddress (in theEmailAddress : String = "") : Boolean
```

To summarize, this operation definition communicates the following:

The + symbol
> Indicates that the addEmailAddress operation is public and is accessible by other objects. The expression inside the parentheses indicates the parameters that hold the values passed to the operation.

The in keyword
> Indicates that the parameter is input and may not be modified by the operation.

theEmailAddress : String = ""
> Indicates that an email address, which is a string with a default value of an empty string, is passed to the operation.

The Boolean keyword
> Indicates that the addEmailAddress operation returns a value of true or false, perhaps indicating whether there is room for the email address to be added to the email address attribute (which holds a maximum of five email addresses).

Figure 3-5 shows the Worker class from Figures 3-1 and 3-2 with its various attribute getter and setter operations. Notice that the getter and setter operations for phone numbers are based on the priority of the phone number such that you specify the priority and set or get the corresponding phone number. Also, notice that the getter operation for email addresses retrieves all of a worker's email addresses, while the setter operation for email addresses simply adds one email address. The create and destroy operations create and destroy worker objects, respectively.

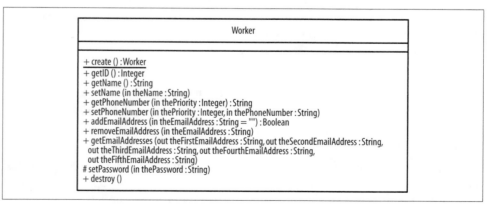

Figure 3-5. Worker class with its operations

Figure 3-6 shows the UnitOfWork class from Figures 3-1 and 3-3 with its various getter and setter operations to set and retrieve attribute values, and with operations to create and destroy UnitOfWork objects.

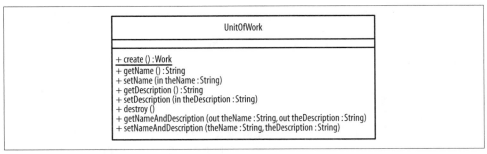

Figure 3-6. *UnitOfWork class with its operations*

Figure 3-7 shows the WorkProduct class from Figures 3-1 and 3-4 with its various getter and setter operations for its attributes and operations to create and destroy work objects. Notice that Figure 3-7 also shows the attributes of the class.

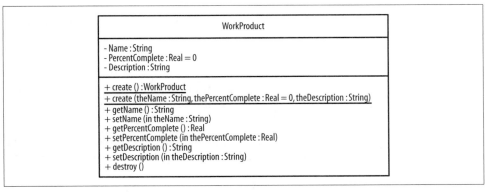

Figure 3-7. *WorkProduct class with its operations*

Operation syntax

In the UML, an operation is described in a class's third compartment using the following UML syntax:

```
visibility operation_name (parameter_list) : return_type
```

in which:

visibility

Is optional, has no default value, and indicates whether the operation is accessible from outside of the class.

It may be one of the following:

+   Public visibility; the operation is accessible from outside its class.

-   Private visibility; the operation is inaccessible from outside its class.

\#   Protected visibility; the operation is accessible by classes that have a generalization relationship (as discussed in Chapter 2) to its class, but is otherwise inaccessible from outside its class.

Figures 3-5, 3-6, and 3-7 show that all the operations are public, except that the operation to set a worker's password is protected so that more specific types of workers or subclasses of the Worker class may use it in whatever manner in which they handle security.

operation_name

> Is the name of the operation you are describing.

parameter_list

> Is optional, has no default value, and is a comma-separated list indicating the parameters that hold the values passed to or received from the operation. Each parameter is shown as a text string having the following syntax:
>
>   kind name : type = default_value

kind

> Is optional, has a default value of in, and may be one of the following:
>
> in
>
> > Indicates the parameter is input-only, and may not be modified by the operation.
>
> out
>
> > Indicates the parameter is output-only, and may be modified by the operation to communicate information to the client that invoked the operation.
>
> inout
>
> > Indicates that the parameter is input and may in turn be modified by the operation to communicate information to the client that invoked the operation.
>
> The type and default value are the same as for an attribute's type and initial value, described in the previous section.

type

> Is optional, has no default value, and indicates the type of data a parameter may hold. If you don't show a type for a parameter, you should omit the colon. The type of a parameter may be another class. In addition, the UML provides the following data types:
>
> Boolean
>
> > A true or false value.
>
> Integer
>
> > An integer number.
>
> Real
>
> > A real number.
>
> String
>
> > A sequence of characters.

default_value

> Is optional, and indicates the initial value of a parameter. By default, a parameter has no initial value. If you do not show an initial value, you should omit the equal symbol (=).

Figure 3-5 shows an initial value for the parameter to the addEmailAddress method.

return_type

> Is optional, has no default value, and indicates the type of data the operation returns to its caller. If you choose not to show the return type of an operation, you should also omit the colon. Your choices for return type are the same as for a parameter type. Many of the operations shown in Figures 3-5 through 3-7 show a return type.

If you prefer, the UML also allows you to show an operation using pseudocode or another language. For example, you can use the syntax of Java, C++, C#, or some other programming language.

If an operation applies to a specific object, it is known as *instance scoped* or *object scoped*. If an operation applies to the class itself, it is known as *class scoped*. Figures 3-5 through 3-7 show that most of the operations are object scoped. The exceptions are the create operations, which are class scoped. The create operations are used to create objects of a class and are known as *constructors*. The destroy operations are used to destroy objects of a class and are known as *destructors*. The create operations are class scoped, because a class is used to create objects of the class; if create were instance scoped, you'd need to somehow create an object before invoking its create operation to create it, which makes no sense. The destroy operation, on the other hand, is object scoped, because it is applied to a specific object that is to be destroyed.

We can combine Figures 3-2 and 3-5 or Figures 3-3 and 3-6 much the way that Figure 3-7 combines the attributes shown in Figure 3-4 with the class's operations. In this way, we can show any combination of attributes and operations based upon what we want to communicate.

> Methods, the actual implementations of operations, are not shown on a class, but may be described using other UML modeling techniques.

Objects

As discussed in Chapter 2, an *object* is a specific concept, or instance of a class, having the characteristics defined by its class, including structural features and behavioral features. For example, the project management system involves various specific concepts, including specific projects, managers, teams, work products, requirements, systems, and so forth. Recall that structural features define what the object knows, and that behavioral features define what the object can do. Structural features included attribute values and links. Behavioral features include operations and methods, which are shared by all the objects of a class. The most crucial aspect of an object is that it has its own identity. No two objects are the same, even if they have the same values for their structural features. For example, even if two worker objects have the same values for their attributes, the objects are unique and have their own identities.

In a UML object diagram, an object is shown as a solid-outline rectangle with two standard compartments separated by horizontal lines. The required top compartment shows the object name followed by a colon followed by the object's class name, and the entire string is fully underlined. Both names are optional, and the colon should only be present if the class name is specified. The optional second compartment shows a list of attributes. The second compartment need only show the specific information you want to communicate using a given diagram; you need not show all of an object's attribute values all the time.

Figure 3-8 shows various objects associated with the classes shown in the previous figures. These objects include the following:

- Nora and Phillip who are workers
- Testing that is a unit of work
- Test that is a work product
- An anonymous unit of work with the name attribute, Implementation
- An anonymous work product with the name attribute, System
- XYZ that is an unspecified object.

Figure 3-8 introduces notation you haven't seen before: some objects have no names and others have no class specified. Objects in a UML diagram that do not have names are referred to as *anonymous objects*. Objects for which a class has not been specified are referred to as *unspecified objects*. You may encounter such notation depending on the specific methodology being used for a project.

Note that the object names in Figure 3-8 are all fully underlined. You'll also see specific attribute values. I'll discuss attribute values further in the next section.

Attribute values

An *attribute value* is the value an object of a class knows for an attribute. In the UML, an attribute value is described in an object's second compartment. For example, each Worker object of the project management system may have a value for its name.

Consider an attribute value for holding a worker's email addresses. You may define it using the following syntax:

```
- EmailAddress [1] : String = "ph@myorg.org"
```

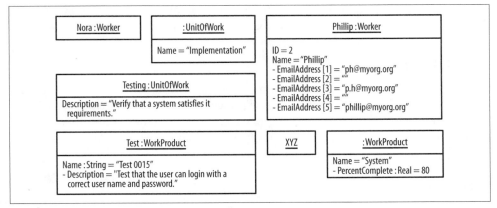

Figure 3-8. Objects

This definition communicates the following:

The - symbol
> Indicates that the email address attribute is private and accessible only by the object.

[1]
> Indicates that this is the first email address value, because there are multiple email address values.

String
> Indicates that the email address is a string of characters.

"ph@myorg.org"
> Indicates the value of the email address attribute.

Following is the general syntax to use for defining attribute values:

```
visibility name [index] : type = value
```

The syntax elements are the same as for the attributes of a class.

Operations

Because the operations and methods of a class are shared by all the objects of the class, operations are not shown on each object. For example, Figure 3-8 shows that both Nora and Phillip are workers, and therefore they share the operations and methods of the Worker class. There is no need to show the operations on each object, as the operations will be unnecessarily repeated each time. To determine the operations of an object, refer to that object's class.

Associations and Links

Class diagrams contain associations, and object diagrams contain links. Both associations and links represent relationships. Associations represent relationships between classes; links represent relationships between objects. The next few sections discuss the UML's representation of associations and links in detail.

Associations

As discussed in Chapter 2, an association defines a type of link and is a general relationship between classes. For example, the project management system involves various general relationships, including manage, lead, execute, input, and output between projects, managers, teams, work products, requirements, and systems. Consider, for example, how a project manager leads a team.

Binary associations

A *binary association* relates two classes. For example, one binary relationship in the project management system is between individual workers and their units of work, and another binary relationship is between individual workers and their work products.

In a UML class diagram, a binary association is shown as a solid-line path connecting the two related classes. A binary association may be labeled with a name. The name is usually read from left to right and top to bottom; otherwise, it may have a small black solid triangle next to it where the point of the triangle indicates the direction in which to read the name, but the arrow is purely descriptive, and the name of the association should be understood by the classes it relates.

Figure 3-9 shows various associations within the project management system using the most basic notation for binary associations. The associations in the figure are as follows:

- A worker is responsible for work products and performs units of work
- Units of work consume work products as input and produce work products as output.

Notice that a binary association should be named using a verb phrase. Recall from Chapter 2 that you discover associations by focusing on verbs.

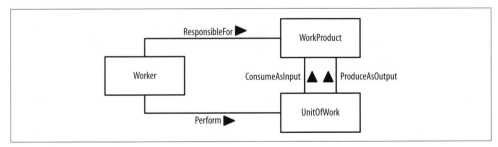

Figure 3-9. Binary associations

N-ary associations

An *n-ary association* relates three or more classes. For example, in the project management system, the use of a worker involves the worker, her units of work, and her associated work products.

In a UML class diagram, an n-ary association is shown as a large diamond with solid-line paths from the diamond to each class. An n-ary association may be labeled with a name. The name is read in the same manner as for binary associations, described in the previous section.

Figure 3-10 shows an n-ary association associated with the project management system using the most basic notation for n-ary associations. This association states that utilization involves workers, units of work, and work products. As with a binary association, an n-ary association is also commonly named using a verb phrase. However, this is not always the case—for example, the n-ary Utilization association shown in Figure 3-10 is described using a noun rather than a verb, because it is named from our perspective rather than the perspective of one of the classes. That is, from our perspective, we want to understand a worker's utilization relative to the other classes. From the worker's perspective, a worker is responsible for work products and performs units of work.

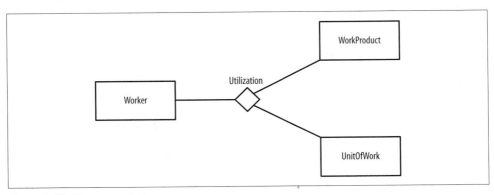

Figure 3-10. N-ary association

Association Classes

Association classes may be applied to both binary and n-ary associations. Similar to how a class defines the characteristics of its objects, including their structural features and behavioral features, an *association class* may be used to define the characteristics of its links, including their structural features and behavioral features. These types of classes are used when you need to maintain information about the relationship itself.

In a UML class diagram, an association class is shown as a class attached by a dashed-line path to its association path in a binary association or to its association diamond in an n-ary association. The name of the association class must match the name of the association.

Figure 3-11 shows association classes for the binary associations in Figure 3-9 using the most basic notation for binary association classes. The association classes track the following information:

- The reason a worker is responsible for a work product
- The reason a worker performs a unit of work
- A description of how a unit of work consumes a work product
- A description of how a unit of work produces a work product.

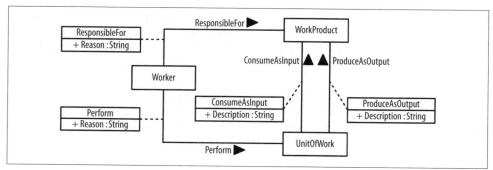

Figure 3-11. Binary association classes

Figure 3-12 shows an association class for the n-ary association in Figure 3-10 using the most basic notation for n-ary association classes. The association class tracks a utilization percentage for workers, their units of work, and their associated work products.

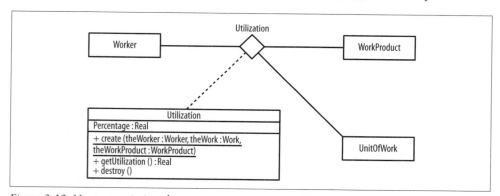

Figure 3-12. N-ary association class

Association Ends

An *association end* is an endpoint of the line drawn for an association, and it connects the association to a class. An association end may include any of the following items to express more detail about how the class relates to the other class or classes in the association:

- Rolename
- Navigation arrow
- Multiplicity specification
- Aggregation or composition symbol
- Qualifier

Rolenames

A *rolename* is optional and indicates the role a class plays relative to the other classes in an association, how the other classes "see" the class or what "face" the class projects to the other classes in the relationship. A rolename is shown near the end of an association attached to a class.

For example, a work product is seen as input by a unit of work where the unit of work is seen as a consumer by the work product; a work product is seen as output by a unit of work where the unit of work is seen as a producer by the work product, as shown in Figure 3-13. I will continue to discuss this figure in the next sections. I particularly captured significant detail in one figure so that you can see how much the UMC enables you to communicate in a figure such as this.

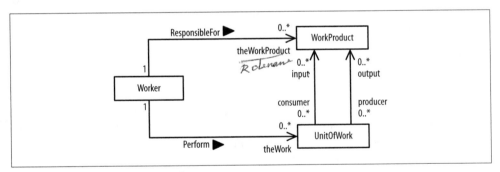

Figure 3-13. Binary association ends

Navigation

Navigation is optional and indicates whether a class may be referenced from the other classes in an association. Navigation is shown as an arrow attached to an association end pointing toward the class in question. If no arrows are present, associations are assumed to be navigable in all directions, and all classes involved in the association may reference one another.

For example, given a worker, you can determine his work products and units of work. Thus, Figure 3-13 shows arrows pointing towards work product and units of work. Given a unit of work, you can determine its input and output work products; but given a work product, you are unable to identify which worker is responsible for it or which units of work reference it as input or output (as shown in Figure 3-13 by the lack of arrows pointing to the Worker class). Figure 3-14 shows navigation arrows applied to an n-ary association. Given a worker, you can reference his work products and units of work to determine his utilization, but given a work product or unit of work, you are unable to determine its utilization by a worker.

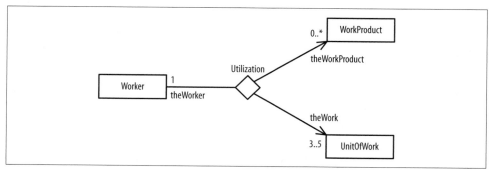

Figure 3-14. N-ary association ends

Multiplicity

Multiplicity (which is optional) indicates how many objects of a class may relate to the other classes in an association. Multiplicity is shown as a comma-separated sequence of the following:

- Integer intervals
- Literal integer values

Intervals are shown as a *lower-bound .. upper-bound* string in which a single asterisk indicates an unlimited range. No asterisks indicate a closed range. For example, 1 means one, 1..5 means one to five, 1, 4 means one or four, 0..* and * mean zero or more (or many), and 0..1 and 0, 1 mean zero or one. There is no default multiplicity for association ends. Multiplicity is simply undefined, unless you specify it. For example:

- A single worker is responsible for zero or more work products.
- A single work product is the responsibility of exactly one worker.
- A single worker performs zero or more units of work.
- A unit of work is performed by exactly one worker.
- A unit of work may input as a consumer zero or more work products and output as a producer zero or more work products.
- A work product may be consumed as input by zero or more units of work and produced as output by zero or more units of work.

All this is shown in Figure 3-13. Continuing the example, utilization may be determined for a single worker who must have three to five units of work and zero or more work products, as shown in Figure 3-14.

To determine the multiplicity of a class, ask yourself how many objects may relate to a single object of the class. The answer determines the multiplicity on the other end of the association. For example, using Figure 3-13, if you have a single worker object, how many work products can a single worker object be responsible for? The answer is zero or more, and that is the multiplicity shown on the diagram next to the WorkProduct class. Using Figure 3-14, if you have a single worker, to how many work products can the single worker be related to determine the worker's utilization? The answer is zero or more, and that is the multiplicity shown on the diagram next to the WorkProduct class.

Another way to determine multiplicity is to ask how many objects of a class may relate to a single object of the class on the other end of an association, or to a single object of each class on the other ends of an n-ary association. The answer determines the multiplicity for the class. For example, using Figure 3-13, how many work products is a single worker responsible for? The answer is zero or more; that is the multiplicity shown on the diagram next to the WorkProduct class. Also, using Figure 3-14, to how many work products is a single worker and a single unit of work related to determine the worker's utilization? The answer is zero or more; that is the multiplicity shown on the diagram next to the WorkProduct class.

Aggregation

Aggregation is whole-part relationship between an *aggregate*, the whole, and its *parts*. This relationship is often known as a *has-a* relationship, because the whole *has* its parts. For example, when you think of workers making up a team, you can say that a team has workers. Aggregation is shown using a hollow diamond attached to the class that represents the whole. This relationship that I've just mentioned between a team and its workers is shown in Figure 3-15. Look for the hollow diamond to the right of the Team class. The filled-in diamonds represent composition, which I'll discuss next. As a UML rule, aggregation is used only with binary associations.

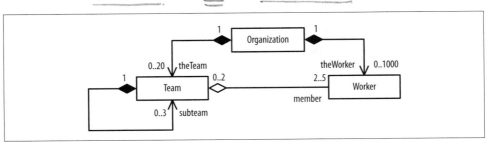

Figure 3-15. Aggregation and composition for associations

Notice in Figure 3-15 that I've done something different with Team. I've created a circular relationship to allow for subteams. Such a circular relationship is known as a *reflexive relationship*, because it relates two objects of the same class.

Composition

Composition, also known as *composite aggregation*, is a whole-part relationship between a *composite* (the whole) and its *parts*, in which the parts must belong only to one whole and the whole is responsible for creating and destroying its parts when it is created or destroyed. This relationship is often known as a *contains-a* relationship, because the whole *contains* its parts. For example, an organization contains teams and workers, and if the organization ceases to exist, its teams and workers also cease to exist. The specific individuals who represent the workers would still exist, but they would no longer be workers of the organization, because the organization would no longer exist. Composition is shown using a filled diamond attached to the class that represents the whole. The relationships between a team, its workers, and an organization are shown in Figure 3-15. The filled-in diamond at the endpoint of the subteam relationship in Figure 3-15 indicates that teams contain their subteams. As a UML rule, composition is used only with binary associations.

Notice how much information is being communicated in Figure 3-15. It shows that an organization may contain 0 to 20 teams and 0 to 1,000 workers. Furthermore, each team has 2 to 5 workers and each worker may be a member of 0 to 2 teams. In addition, a team may contain 0 to 3 subteams.

To determine if you should use an aggregation or composition, ask yourself a few questions. First, if the classes are related to one another, use an association. Next, if one class is part of the other class, which is the whole, use aggregation; otherwise, use an association. For example, Figure 3-15 shows that workers are part of a team and organization, teams are part of an organization, and subteams are part of teams. Finally, if the part must belong to one whole only, and the whole is responsible for creating and destroying its parts, use composition; otherwise, simply use aggregation. For example, Figure 3-15 shows that a team and worker must belong to one organization only, and the organization is responsible for determining (or creating and destroying) its teams and workers. It also shows that a subteam must belong to one team only, and the team is responsible for determining (or creating and destroying) its subteams. If this is unclear, keep things simple and use associations without aggregation or composition.

Composition also may be shown by graphically nesting classes, in which a nested class's multiplicity is shown in its upper-right corner and its rolename is indicated in front of its class name. Separate the rolename from the class name using a colon. Figure 3-16 uses the graphical nesting of teams and workers in organizations to communicate the same information as shown in Figure 3-15.

Figure 3-17 uses the graphical nesting of subteams within teams to communicate the same information as Figures 3-15 and 3-16. The result is a nested class inside a nested class.

Qualifiers

A *qualifier* is an attribute of an association class that reduces the multiplicity across an association. For example, Figure 3-13 shows that multiplicity between work

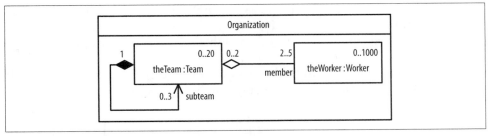

Figure 3-16. Alternate form of composition for associations

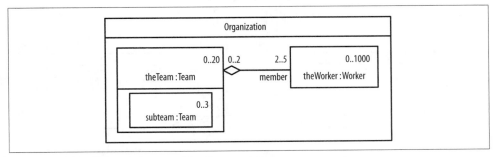

Figure 3-17. Doubly nested composition for associations

products and units of work is zero or more for both associations; that is, there may be many work products associated with a single unit of work and there may be many units of work associated with a single work product. Rather than simply say that there are "many" objects involved in the relationship, you can communicate a more finite number.

You can reduce the multiplicity between work products and units of work by asking yourself what you need to know about a unit of work so that you can define a more specific multiplicity—one that isn't unbounded on the high-end. Likewise, you can ask yourself the same question about the association between work product and units of work. If you have a work product and the name of a unit of work, you can determine whether a relationship exists between the two; likewise, if you have a unit of work and the name of a work product, you can determine whether a relationship exists between those two. The trick is to document precisely what information is needed so you can identify the objects on the other end of the relationship. This is where the qualifier comes into play.

Essentially, a qualifier is a piece of information used as an index to find the objects on the other end of an association. A qualifier is shown as a small rectangle attached to a class where an object of the class, together with a value for the qualifier, reduces the multiplicity on the other end of the association. Qualifiers have the same notation as attributes, have no initial values, and must be attributes of the association or the class on the other end of the association.

The relationships between work products and units of work and their qualifiers are shown in Figure 3-18. The qualifiers indicate that a work product with the name of a unit of work may identify a unit of work, and that a unit of work with the name of a work product may identify a work product. Notice that I've reduced the multiplicity of 0..* shown in Figure 3-13 to 0..1 in Figure 3-18. The qualifier enables me to do this. As a UML rule, qualifiers are used only with binary associations.

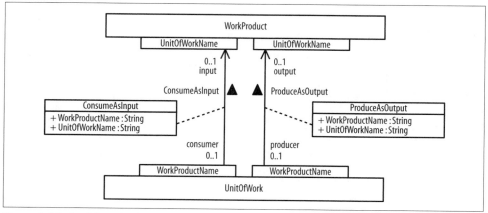

Figure 3-18. Qualifiers for associations

Links

As discussed in Chapter 2, a *link* is a specific relationship between objects. For example, the project management system involves various specific relationships, including specific manage, lead, execute, input, output, and other relationships between specific projects, managers, teams, work products, requirements, systems, and so forth. A link is an instance of an association, and the UML supports different types of links that correspond to the different types of associations.

The general rules for representing links in a UML diagram are as follows:

- Label links with their association names, and underline the names to show that they are specific instances of their respective associations.
- Ensure that link ends are consistent with their corresponding association ends.
- Translate association multiplicity into one or more specific links between specific objects.

The next few sections show how to apply these rules to the various link types.

Binary links

A *binary link*, which is a specific relationship between two objects, is shown as a solid-line path connecting the two objects in a UML object diagram. For example, a specific worker is related to specific units of work and work products in the project management system. A link may have its association name shown near the path (fully underlined), but links do not have instance names.

Figure 3-19 shows various objects associated with the classes shown in Figure 3-13 and the association classes shown in Figure 3-11. Additionally, Figure 3-19 includes several link objects. Figure 3-19 describes an anonymous worker that performs a project—a unit of work—that consumes a Problem Statement work product and produces a system work product. ResponsibleFor and Performed are two links in Figure 3-19.

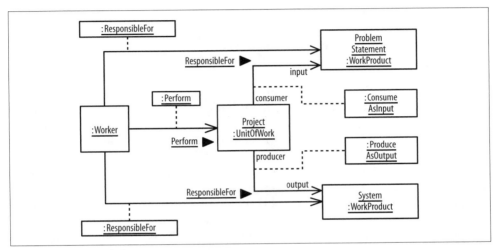

Figure 3-19. Binary links

The only difference between a binary link and a binary association is that the binary link is specific, and thus has its association name underlined.

N-ary links

An *n-ary link*, a relationship between three or more objects, is shown as a large diamond with solid-line paths from the diamond to each object in a UML object diagram. For example, the utilization of a specific worker involves the worker, the worker's specific units of work, and the worker's specific work products in the project management system. A link may have its association name shown near the path, and because a link is specific, its association name should be fully underlined. However, links do not have instance names. As a UML rule, aggregation, composition, and qualifiers may not be used with n-ary links.

Figure 3-20 shows various objects associated with the classes shown in Figure 3-14 and the association classes shown in Figure 3-12. Additionally, Figure 3-20 includes a link object named Utilization. Figure 3-20 describes the utilization of an anonymous team, its work, and work products.

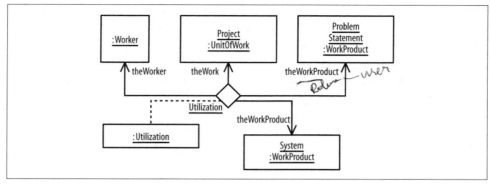

Figure 3-20. N-ary link

Link Objects

A *link object* is a specific instance of an association class, and thus has all the characteristics, including structural and behavioral features, defined by the association class. Structural features include attribute values and perhaps other links. Behavioral features include operations and methods, which are shared by all the links of an association class. Whenever an association has a related association class, each of its links has a corresponding link object. This link object defines attribute values for the link's structural features. In addition, the behavioral features defined by the link's association class apply to the link objects. In a UML object diagram, a link object is shown as an object rectangle attached by a dashed-line path to its link path in a binary link, or attached to its link diamond in an n-ary link. As with all UML elements representing specific objects or links, link object names should be fully underlined.

Figure 3-19 shows link objects for the binary associations in Figure 3-13, and Figure 3-20 shows a link object for the n-ary association in Figure 3-14.

Link Ends

A *link end*, similar to an association end, is an endpoint of a link and connects the link to an object. A link end may show its association end's rolename, navigation arrow, aggregation or composition symbol, and values for its association end's qualifiers.

Rolenames

A link end's rolename must match its association end's rolename. For example, Figure 3-13 shows that a Worker is responsible for a WorkProduct. The specific association used is ResponsibleFor; this same association name is used again in Figure 3-19 to describe the specific links between a specific Worker and the two specific work products: ProblemStatement and System.

Navigation

Likewise, a link end's navigation must match its association end's navigation. For example, the arrows on the two ResponsibleFor links in Figure 3-19 both point to instances of WorkProduct. This is consistent with Figure 3-13, which shows the arrow for the ResponsibleFor association pointing to the WorkProduct class.

Multiplicity

Multiplicity is shown only on association ends. This is because an association describes the multiplicity between two or more classes of objects. A link however, is between specific objects. Thus, in an object diagram, multiplicity manifests itself in terms of a specific number of links pointing to a specific number of discrete objects. For example, the multiplicity shown in Figure 3-13 indicates that a Worker object may be responsible for zero to many (0..*) WorkProduct objects. In Figure 3-19, two specific WorkProduct objects are shown. Figure 3-19 is specific, and the specific multiplicity in this case is two: the specific Worker object is responsible for two specific WorkProduct objects.

Aggregation

Aggregation is shown using a hollow diamond, as shown in Figures 3-21 through 3-23. Figure 3-21 shows three teams named Eagle, Falcon, and Hawk. Jonathan, Andy, Nora, and Phillip are on the Eagle team, while Nora and Phillip are also on the Hawk team.

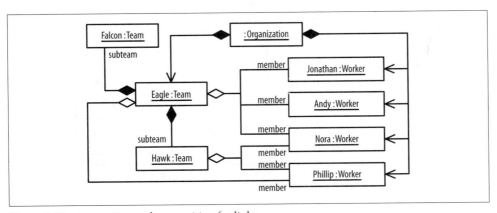

Figure 3-21. Aggregation and composition for links

Composition

Composition may be shown using a filled diamond or graphical nesting, as in Figure 3-21. Figure 3-21 shows that the two teams, Falcon and Hawk, are subteams of the Eagle team. In addition, the filled-in diamond next to the Organization class indicates that all the individuals on these teams belong to the same organization, and that the Eagle team itself belongs to the organization.

Figure 3-22 uses the graphical nesting of teams and workers in organizations to communicate the same information as Figure 3-21.

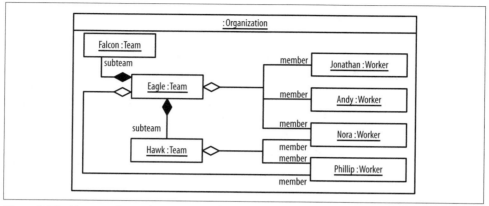

Figure 3-22. Alternate form of composition for links

Figure 3-23 uses the graphical nesting of subteams in teams to communicate the same information as Figures 3-21 and 3-22.

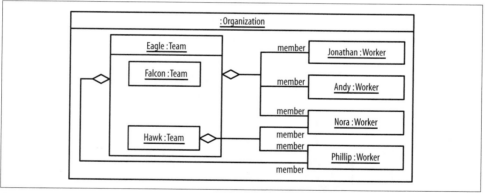

Figure 3-23. Doubly nested composition for links

Qualifiers

Values for link qualifiers have the same notation as for object attribute values. Figure 3-24 shows how qualifier values associate a project with its problem statement (named Problem Statement) and system (named PM-System).

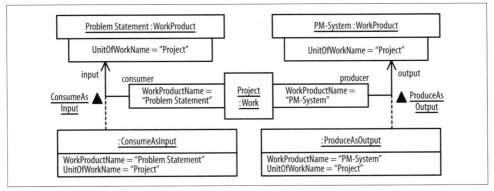

Figure 3-24. Qualifier values for links

Types, Implementation Classes, and Interfaces

The kinds of classes discussed thus far are known as *undifferentiated classes*, and are commonly used during design activities within a development process. You can also differentiate between three different kinds of classes, called *differentiated classes*. These include:

- Types
- Implementation classes
- Interfaces

These differentiated classes closely relate to different activities in the development process. The next few sections discuss these differentiated classes.

Types

A *type* is a class that may have attributes, associations, and operations, but does not have any methods. A type defines a role an object may play relative to other objects, similar to how a rolename indicates the role a class plays relative to other classes in an association. For example, a Worker object may play the role of a project manager, resource manager, human resource, or system administrator. A type is shown as a class marked with the type keyword. These types of workers are shown in Figure 3-25.

Types are commonly used during analysis activities within a development process to identify the kinds of objects a system may require. You can think of types as conceptual classes, because they are ideas for possible classes. Also, because types do not have methods and represent roles only, they do not have instances.

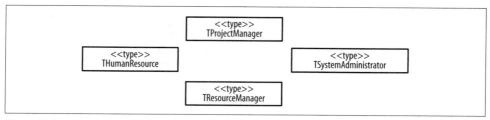

Figure 3-25. Types

Types may be used with binary and n-ary association and link ends. A comma-separated list of one or more type names may be placed following a rolename to indicate the roles a class or object plays in the relationship. Separate the rolename from the list of types using a colon. If no rolename is used, the type names are placed following a colon.

Figure 3-26 uses the types from Figure 3-25 to update Figure 3-13. It shows the various roles a worker may play relative to work products and units of work. A worker may be a project manager, resource manager, human resource, and system administrator.

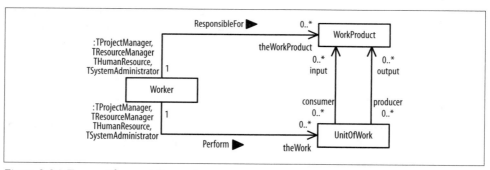

Figure 3-26. Types with association ends

Implementation Classes

An *implementation class* is a class that may have attributes, associations, operations, and methods. An implementation class defines the physical implementation of objects of a class. For example, if you were to implement our classes in a database management system, the Worker class might be implemented as an employee table, the WorkProduct class might be implemented as an artifact table, and the UnitOfWork class might be implemented as work order table. An implementation class is shown as a class marked with the implementationClass keyword. The three implementation classes just mentioned are shown in Figure 3-27.

Implementation classes are commonly used during the later part of design and during implementation activities within a development process to identify how objects are implemented for a system. You can think about implementation classes as physical "code" classes because, they are physical implementations of classes.

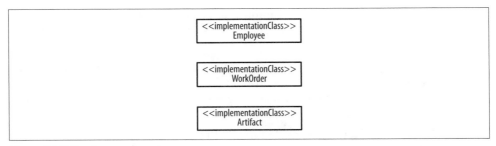

Figure 3-27. Implementation classes

Interfaces

An *interface* is a class that may have operations but may not have attributes, associations, or methods. An interface defines a service or contract as a collection of public operations. For example, a project manager must be able to initiate and terminate a project, plan and manage a project while leading a team, and so forth. A resource manager must be able to assign and unassign human resources to and from a team. A work product must be producible and consumable; it is produced by being created or written, and consumed by being read or destroyed. Interfaces can be used to define these collections of operations.

An interface is shown as a class marked with the `interface` keyword, and because interfaces don't have attributes, the second compartment is always empty and, therefore, not shown. An interface also may be shown as a small circle with the interface name placed near the symbol and the operations of the interface not shown. Examples of both interface representations are shown in Figure 3-28.

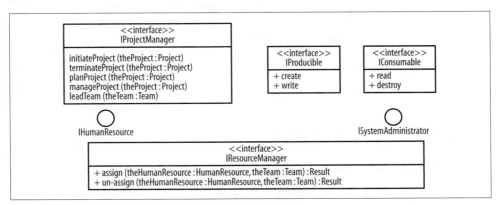

Figure 3-28. Interfaces

Interfaces are commonly used during analysis and design activities within a development process to identify services that classes and their objects provide. You can think of interfaces as application programming interfaces (APIs), because they define a collection of operations that are commonly used together and thus define a more general service. Because interfaces do not have methods but merely represent services, they do not have instances.

Interfaces may be used with binary and n-ary association and link ends to indicate the services (or interfaces) that a class provides in the relationship. Begin with a rolename followed by a colon, then add a comma-separated list of one or more interface names, as shown in Figure 3-29.

Figure 3-29 uses the interfaces from Figure 3-28 to update Figure 3-26. It shows the various services a work product provides to units of work, including an interface for consumption of the work product and an interface for production of the work product. It also shows the various interfaces a worker provides in association with work products and units of work. Interfaces and types may be listed together, but types are more commonly used during analysis activities, while interfaces are more commonly used during analysis and design activities. Because both interfaces and types may be used during analysis and design, it is very important to have a standard naming convention. For example, one convention is to prefix interfaces with an I and to prefix types with a T.

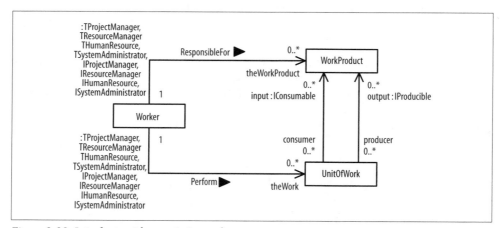

Figure 3-29. Interfaces with association ends

Generalizations, Realizations, and Dependencies

While it is common to use types during analysis activities, interfaces during analysis activities and design activities, undifferentiated classes during design activities, and implementation classes during the later part of design and during implementation activities, how are all these elements related? Generalizations, realizations, and dependencies, called *specialized relationships*, address the question of how undifferentiated and differentiated classes are related. The next few sections discuss these relationships.

Generalizations

A generalization between a more general element and a more specific element of the same kind indicates that the more specific element receives the attributes, associations and other relationships, operations, and methods from the more general element. The two elements must be of the same kind. For example, a generalization relationship can be between two types but not between a type and an interface. Generalization relationships may exist for the following kinds of elements:

- Types
- Undifferentiated classes
- Implementation classes
- Interfaces

A generalization is shown as a solid-line path from the more specific element to the more general element, with a large hollow triangle at the end of the path connected to the more general element. You'll see examples of this as I discuss each specific type of generalization in the following sections.

Types

The project manager, human resource, and system administrator types shown earlier in Figure 3-25 are specific types of human resources. You can model a generalization of these three types to factor out structure and behavior common to all. A generalization between types allows us to reuse a type's attributes, associations, and operations to define a new type. Figure 3-30 shows that the THumanResource type is a generalization of TProjectManager, TSystemAdministrator, and TResourceManager.

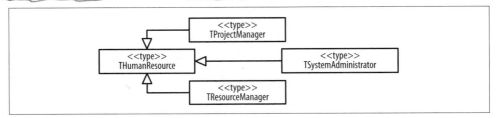

Figure 3-30. Generalizations between types

Because a generalization between a more general type and a more specific type indicates that the more specific type is a specialized form of the more general type, those classes that may play the roles of the more specific type may also play the roles of the more general type. Therefore, Figure 3-30 shows that those objects that play the specific roles of project manager, resource manager, and system administrator may also each play the more general role of a human resource.

Undifferentiated classes

The Worker class shown in Figure 3-26 may have a more specialized undifferentiated class of human resource, which itself has more specialized undifferentiated classes, including project managers, resource managers, and system administrators. You can nest generalization relationships for undifferentiated classes as well as types, interfaces, and differentiated classes. For example, project managers, resource managers, and system administrators all could be specializations of a human resource. A human resource, on the other hand, could be a specialization of a worker, or a worker could be a generalization of a human resource. A generalization between undifferentiated classes allows us to reuse a class's attributes, associations, operations, and methods to define a new undifferentiated class. The relationships among the undifferentiated classes just mentioned are shown in Figure 3-31.

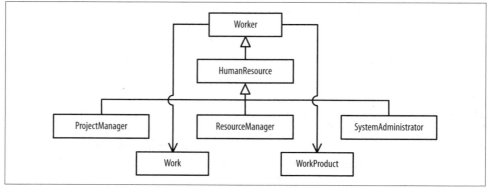

Figure 3-31. Generalizations between classes

Figure 3-30 shows three generalization paths, while Figure 3-31 combines three generalization paths from the ProjectManager, ResourceManager, and SystemAdministrator classes into one path that connects to the HumanResource class. Whenever several paths of the same kind connect to a single element, the UML allows you to combine those paths into a single path as shown in this figure. Also, when paths cross but do not connect, the UML allows you to show this with a small, semicircular jog by one of the paths, as shown for the associations between the Worker class and the UnitOfWork and WorkProduct classes. The jog indicates that the line with the jog does not connect in any way with the other line passing through the jog.

Given a specific class, any immediately more general classes are called *parents* or *super-classes*. Any immediately more specific classes are called *children* or *subclasses*. General classes that are not parents (i.e., not immediately more general) are called *ancestors*. More specific classes that are not children (i.e., not immediately more specific) are called *descendants*. Therefore, Figure 3-31 shows that the Worker class is the parent of the HumanResource class, and the ProjectManager, ResourceManager, and SystemAdministrator classes are the children of the HumanResource class. It also shows that the Worker class is an ancestor of the ProjectManager, ResourceManager, and SystemAdministrator classes, and that these classes are descendants of the Worker class.

Because a generalization between two undifferentiated classes indicates that objects of the more specific undifferentiated class are more specialized objects of the more general undifferentiated class, objects of the more specific undifferentiated class may be substituted for objects of the more general undifferentiated class. Therefore, Figure 3-31 shows that project manager, resource manager, and system administrator objects may be substituted for human resource objects.

Implementation classes

A generalization between implementation classes allows us to reuse an implementation class's attributes, associations, operations, and methods to define a new implementation class. Earlier, I raised the possibility of implementing the classes shown in Figure 3-27 as database tables. In such a case, the three implementation classes in Figure 3-27 could all be specialized classes of a database table class. Figure 3-32 shows this by making Employee, WorkOrder, and Artifact into specializations of a more general DatabaseTable class.

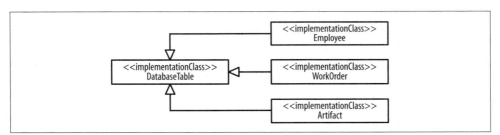

Figure 3-32. Generalizations between implementation classes

Because a generalization between a more general implementation class and a more specific implementation class indicates that objects of the more specific implementation class are specialized objects of the general implementation class, objects of the specific implementation class may be substituted for objects of the general implementation class. Therefore, Figure 3-32 shows that employee, work order, and artifact objects may be substituted for database table objects.

Interfaces

The project manager, human resource, and system administrator interfaces shown in Figure 3-28 are more specific versions of the human resource interface. A generalization between interfaces allows us to reuse an interface's operations to define a new interface. The relationships among the interfaces just mentioned are shown in Figure 3-33.

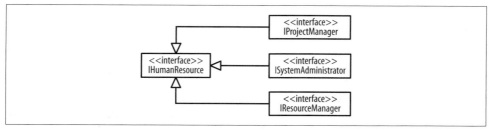

Figure 3-33. Generalizations between interfaces

Because a generalization between a more general interface and a more specific interface indicates that the more specific interface is a specialized form of the more general interface, those classes that provide the service defined by the more specific interface may also provide the service defined by the more general interface. Therefore, Figure 3-33 shows that those objects that provide the project manager, human resource, and system administrator interfaces also provide the human resource interface.

Realizations

A *realization* from a source element (called the *realization element*) to a target element (called the *specification element*) indicates that the source element supports at least all the operations of the target element without necessarily having to support any attributes or associations of the target element. For example, an undifferentiated class or implementation class may play the role defined by a type and may provide the service defined by an interface, if the class supports the operations defined by the type and interface. A realization allows us to reuse the operations of types and interfaces where a realization element is said to *realize* its specification elements.

A realization is shown as a dashed-line path from the source element to the target element, with a large hollow triangle at the end of the path connected to the target element. When the target element is an interface shown as a small circle, the realization is shown as a solid-line path connecting the source and interface.

Undifferentiated classes

Figure 3-29 shows a list of types and interfaces that the Worker class supports. Based on Figure 3-29, Figure 3-34 shows that the Worker class realizes those types and interfaces. The source element is the Worker class, and the other elements are the targets. Figure 3-29 shows how interfaces and types are used in the various associations between the Worker class and other classes, while Figure 3-34 shows that the Worker class explicitly realizes these interfaces and types independent of how they are used in relationships.

Based on Figure 3-29, Figure 3-35 shows the interfaces work products realize. The source element is the WorkProduct class and the other elements are the targets.

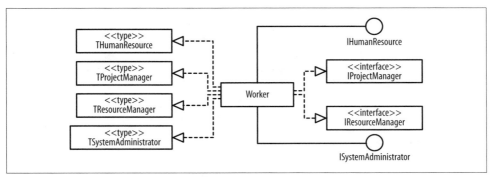

Figure 3-34. Realizations for the Worker class

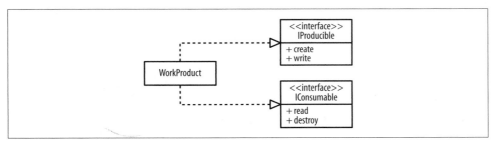

Figure 3-35. Realizations for the WorkProduct class

Because a realization from a source class to a target element indicates that objects of the source class support all the operations of the target element, objects of the source class may be substituted for objects of other classes that also realize the same target element. Therefore, Figure 3-34 shows that a worker object may be substituted for objects of other classes that realize the same types and interfaces as the worker object, and objects of other classes that realize the same types and interfaces as the worker object may be substituted for worker objects. That is, if two objects realize the same type or interface, they may be substituted for one another. Figure 3-35 illustrates this.

Implementation classes

Based on Figure 3-27, Figure 3-36 shows that the Worker class may be implemented as an employee table, the WorkProduct class may be implemented as an artifact table, and the UnitOfWork class may be implemented as work order table, if you are to implement your classes in a database management system. This is indicated with the realization relationships between the Employee implementation class realizing the Worker class, the WorkOrder implementation class realizing the UnitOfWork class, and the Artifact implementation class realizing the WorkProduct class.

When an implementation class realizes an undifferentiated class, it must also realize the types and interfaces that the undifferentiated class realizes; otherwise, it could not play the roles defined by the undifferentiated class's types and provide the services defined by the undifferentiated class's interfaces.

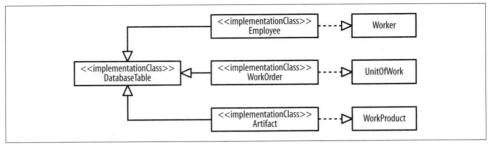

Figure 3-36. Realizations of undifferentiated classes by implementation classes

Based on Figures 3-36 and 3-34, Figure 3-37 shows the types and interfaces the Employee implementation class realizes.

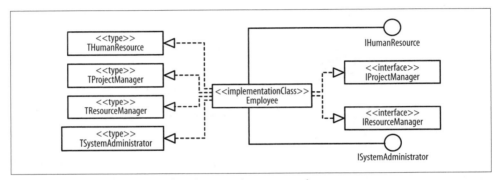

Figure 3-37. Realizations for the Employee implementation class

Based on Figures 3-36 and 3-35, Figure 3-38 shows the interfaces the Artifact implementation class realizes.

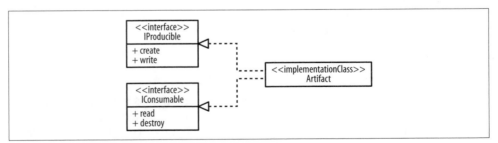

Figure 3-38. Realizations for the Artifact implementation class

Because a realization from a source class to a target element indicates that objects of the source class support all the operations of the target element, objects of the source class may be substituted for objects of other classes that also realize the same target element. Therefore, Figure 3-37 shows that an employee object may be substituted for objects of other classes that realize the same types and interfaces as the employee object, and objects of other classes that realize the same types and interfaces as the employee object may be substituted for employee objects. Figure 3-38 shows the same for an artifact object.

Dependencies

A *dependency* from a source element (called the *client*) to a target element (called the *supplier*) indicates that the source element uses or depends on the target element; if the target element changes, the source element may require a change. For example, a UnitOfWork uses the IConsumable interface as a consumer and uses the IProducible interface as a producer; if either interface changes, the UnitOfWork may require a change. Figure 3-29 shows the interfaces used by UnitOfWork.

A dependency is shown as a dashed-line path from the source element to the target element. The dependency may be marked with the use keyword; however, the keyword is often omitted because the meaning is evident from how the dependency is used. Also, notice that a dependency does not have a large hollow triangle at the end of the path, but has an open arrow.

Based on Figure 3-29, Figure 3-39 shows the dependencies between units of work and work products. Notice that a realization may be shown as a dependency marked with the realize keyword, as shown in Figure 3-39 between the WorkProduct class and the IProducible interface.

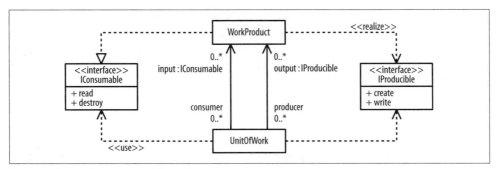

Figure 3-39. Realizations and dependencies

Figure 3-40 shows the dependencies between the interfaces discussed in this chapter and the parameter and return types for their operations. For example, IProjectManager must depend on Project, because many of its operations take a Project object as a parameter.

Packages and Subsystems

As a model may have hundreds (if not thousands) of model elements, how do you organize the elements that make up a system and their relationships? And how do

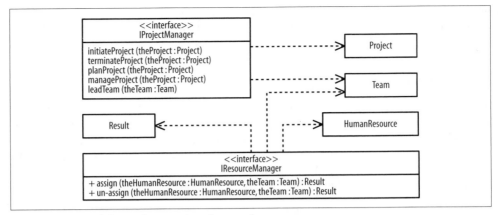

Figure 3-40. Dependencies between interfaces and return types

you use this information to determine how best to develop the system while considering technical trade-offs concerning the system, including which elements may be developed in parallel, which elements may be purchased rather than built, and which elements may be reused? Packages and subsystems, called *model management elements*, address these questions.

Packages

A *package* is a grouping and organizing element in which other elements reside, which must be uniquely named. In the UML, packages are used in a manner similar to the way directories and folders in an operating system group and organize files. For example, the project management system may be decomposed into a collection of classes organized into packages as follows:

Utility
> Date, time, and other utility classes

Workers
> The Worker class and any other worker-related classes in which the Worker class is contained inside of a package named Generic

Generic
> Generic classes such as the Worker class and any other worker-related classes

Work Units
> The UnitOfWork class and any other work-related classes

Work Products
> The WorkProduct class and any other work product–related classes

User Interface
> A package housing classes responsible for providing a user interface through which users may interact with the system

`Business Processing`

A package housing classes responsible for implementing business functionality

`Data`

A package housing classes responsible for implementing data storage functionality

Packages allow us to partition our system into logical groups and then to relate these logical groups; otherwise, it could become overwhelming to work with every class and its relationship at once. A package is shown as a large rectangle with a small rectangle or "tab" attached to its top, left side. The packages in the previous list, together with their relationships, are shown in Figure 3-41.

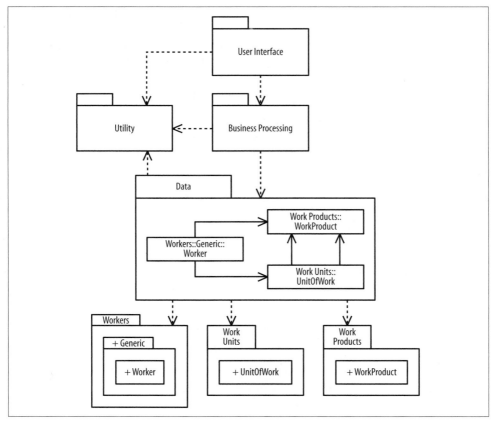

Figure 3-41. Packages

You can show the name of a package inside of its large rectangle when the package contents are not shown; otherwise, when the package contents are shown in the large rectangle, you should show the name of a package inside its tab. In Figure 3-41, you see that the User Interface, Utility, and Business Processing packages don't show their contents, while all the other packages do show some of their contents.

Thus, the User Interface, Utility, and Business Processing packages have their package names within the large rectangle, whereas the other packages have their names in their respective tabs. Each element inside a package may have a visibility symbol indicating whether the element is accessible from outside its package (i.e., is public). Figure 3-41 shows that the Worker, UnitOfWork, and WorkProduct classes are public. The Generic package located inside of the Workers package is also public.

A dependency from a source package to a target package indicates that the contents of the source package use the contents of the target package. Figure 3-41 shows that the Data package uses the Workers, Work Units, and Work Products packages. It also shows that the User Interface, Business Processing, and Data packages use the Utility package, while the User Interface package uses the Business Processing package, which in turn uses the Data package.

A package defines a *namespace*, a part of a model in which a name must be unique. An element shown in a package is most likely defined in that package if it is simply named. For example, the Work Units package in Figure 3-41 defines one public class named UnitOfWork. You can show the UnitOfWork class in other packages to indicate that those packages use the class, in which case you qualify the class name with the path to the package in which the class is defined. Such a fully qualified name is referred to as a pathname. The *pathname* of an element is a sequence of package names linked together and separated by double colons (::), followed by the name of the element. The sequence of package names starts from the outermost package level and works its way down to the package containing the element in question. Figure 3-41 shows that the Data package uses the following:

Workers::Generic::Worker
> The Worker class located inside the Generic package, which is nested inside the Workers package

Work Units::UnitOfWork
> The UnitOfWork class located inside the Work Units package

Work Products::WorkProduct
> The WorkProduct class located inside the Work Products package

Subsystems

Recall that a system is an organized collection of elements that may be recursively decomposed into smaller subsystems and eventually into nondecomposable primitive elements. For example, the project management system may be decomposed into the following:

- A user interface subsystem responsible for providing a user interface through which users may interact with the system

- A business processing subsystem responsible for implementing business functionality

- A data subsystem responsible for implementing data storage functionality

The primitive elements would be the various classes that are used in these subsystems and ultimately in the whole system. While a package simply groups elements, a subsystem groups elements that together provide services such that other elements may access only those services and none of the elements themselves. And while packages allow us to partition our system into logical groups and relate these logical groups, subsystems allow us to consider what services these logical groups provide to one another.

A subsystem is shown as a package marked with the subsystem keyword. The large package rectangle may have three standard compartments shown by dividing the rectangle with a vertical line and then dividing the area to the left of this line into two compartments with a horizontal line. Figure 3-42 shows how a Data subsystem for our project management system might look. The subsystem's operations, specification elements, and interfaces describe the services the subsystem provides, and are the only services accessible by other elements outside the subsystem.

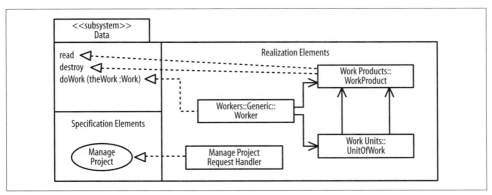

Figure 3-42. A subsystem's representation in the UML

The upper-left compartment shows a list of operations that the subsystem realizes. The lower-left compartment may be labeled "Specification Elements" and shows specification elements that the subsystem realizes. For example, any use cases that the subsystem provides are specification elements that the subsystem must realize. The right compartment may be labeled "Realization Elements" and shows elements inside the subsystem that realize the subsystem's operations and specification elements as well as any interfaces that the subsystem provides. You can modify this general notation by rearranging compartments, combining compartments, or completely suppressing one or more compartments. Any element may be used as a specification or realization element, because a realization simply indicates that the realization element supports at least all the operations of the specification element without necessarily having to support any attributes or associations of the specification element.

Figure 3-43 uses subsystems to refine Figure 3-41. The Business Processing and Data packages from Figure 3-41 are now subsystems. The Business Processing subsystem provides an interface that is used by the User Interface package. The Business Processing subsystem itself uses the Data subsystem and the IProducible interface provided by the Data subsystem. The Data subsystem realizes the IProducible interface, which is outside the subsystem itself, various operations, and the Manage Project use case that was discussed in Chapter 2. The use case is the oval in the specification element's compartment. The realization elements of the Data subsystem realize the read, destroy, and doWork operations, the use case, and the operations of the IProducible interface.

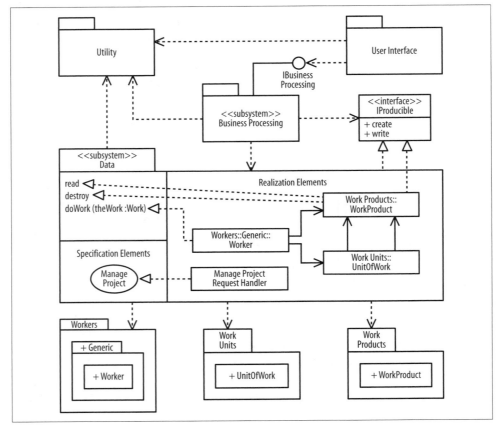

Figure 3-43. Subsystems

Notice in Figure 3-43 that the User Interface package does not use the Business Processing package as shown in Figure 3-41, but instead uses the IBusinessProcessing interface provided by the Business Processing subsystem. This use of an interface allows us to focus on the service that the User Interface package uses rather than on the package providing the service. If you focus on the fact that the User Interface package uses the Business Processing package, you are unaware of the exact operations the User Interface package requires from the Business Processing package; if there is a change to the Business Processing package, you would have to expend significant effort to determine whether the change requires modifying the User Interface package. By focusing on the service that the User Interface package uses rather than the package providing the service, you are aware of the exact operations used from the package providing the service; only if there is a change to the service or to those operations do you have to expend effort to determine whether the change requires modifying the User Interface package. Rather than having to consider all the operations available inside the Business Processing package to determine whether changes to that package impact the User Interface package, you need only look at a subset of those operations: the subset defined by the IBusinessProcess interface. Similarly, notice how the Business Processing package uses the Data package in Figure 3-41, but the Business Processing subsystem uses the operations, specification elements, and IProducible interface provided by the Data subsystem in Figure 3-43.

Figure 3-43 shows the major elements that make up the project management system and the relationships between them. Using packages, subsystems, interfaces, and their relationships, you can more readily consider which elements may be developed in parallel, which elements may be purchased rather than built, and which elements may be reused. It is possible to address these issues with classes and their relationships, but because a system may have many classes, it can easily become overwhelming to work with such granularity. You could also address these issues by using packages and their dependencies, but packages don't offer services. Packages simply capture the major elements that make up a system and not the services that are being used from a package. Thus, you must focus on all the contents of a package rather than on the services used by elements that depend on the package. However, by using packages, subsystems, interfaces, and their relationships, you can more readily address the issues listed earlier, because you capture the major elements making up the system, as well as the services that are provided and required for these elements to work together to provide the functionality of the system.

Because a subsystem's operations, specification elements, and interfaces describe the services the subsystem provides, which are the only services accessible by other elements outside the subsystem, any collection of subsystems may be developed in parallel, because any interdependencies between them rely only on their services. For example, you may develop the Data subsystem and Business Processing subsystem in parallel, because any elements that use these subsystems always use the defined services.

Because a subsystem's services are fully specified, you can attempt to search for and purchase (rather than build) a subsystem that provides the same services. For example, you may not have enough funding to build the Data subsystem, but because you know the services of the subsystem, you can attempt to search and purchase a similar subsystem that offers the same services.

Because a subsystem's services are fully specified, you can reuse the subsystem whenever you require similar services. For example, whenever you require services defined by the IBusinessProcessing interface, you can reuse any subsystem that provides the interface; whenever you require services defined by the IProducible interface, the read operation, the destroy operation, the doWork operation, or the Manage Project use case, you can reuse any subsystem that provides any of these services.

Exercises

1. Describe Figure 3-44: identify the class and describe its attributes and operations.

Figure 3-44. Report class

2. Describe Figure 3-45: identify the object and describe its attribute values.

3. Describe Figure 3-46: identify the classes and their associations.

    Update the diagram stepwise to show the following details. After each step, check your answers against the solutions shown in Appendix B:

    a. When a worker has a skill, the years of experience is maintained for the relationship.

    b. A worker may have another worker as a manager, and a worker who is a manager must manage five or more workers. Given a manager, you can determine whom she manages, but given a worker, you are unable to determine who his manager is.

Figure 3-45. Report object

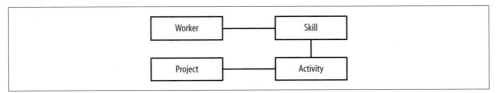

Figure 3-46. Workers, skills, projects, and activities

c. An activity may have no more than one previous activity and any number of next activities. Using these rolenames, we can show how activities are ordered. Given an activity, you can only determine its next activities (if it has any) but not its previous activity (it if has one). This is similar to how a team may be made of subteams in that you have to have a team before you can have a subteam.

d. A worker is not simply associated with a set of skills, but a worker has skills. Specifically, a worker must have three or more skills, and any number of workers may have the same skill.

e. A project is not simply associated with a set of activities, but a project contains activities. Specifically, a project must have one or more activities, and an activity must belong only to one project.

f. Projects and activities are specific types of work.

4. Describe Figure 3-47: identify the classes and their associations.

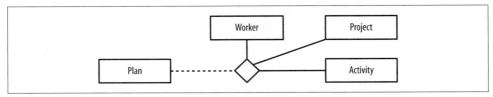

Figure 3-47. Plans, workers, projects, and activities

Update the diagram stepwise (check your answers after each step in Appendix B):

a. A plan pertains to a single project and involves one or more workers and one or more activities.

b. A worker may have zero or more plans, and a plan must belong to a single worker.

c. Each plan contains a single schedule. Given a plan, you can determine its schedule, but given a schedule, you are unable to determine the plan to which it pertains.

d. When an activity is on a schedule, it is called a scheduled activity, and the start date, end date, and duration are maintained for the scheduled activity. Each schedule may have zero or more activities, but an activity must be associated with a single schedule.

e. A milestone, a major point in project, is a special type of scheduled activity where it has zero or more work products that have a specific status. A milestone has any number of work products associated with it, and a work product may be related to any number of milestones.

5. Given the solutions to questions 3 and 4, create a diagram to communicate the following:

a. Nora manages Andy and Jonathan, who are all workers. You are interested in the following skills: project management, requirements gathering, analysis, design, implementation, testing, deployment, Extensible Markup Language (XML), Structured Query Language (SQL), Java, C#, and C++. Nora has 10 years of project management skills, 5 years of analysis skills, and 3 years of design skills. Andy has 3 years of experience in each of the following skills: XML, SQL, Java, and C#. Jonathan has 10 years of experience in SQL, 5 years of experience in C++, 2 years of experience in Java, and 6 months of experience in C#.

b. A project named Eagle contains the following activities: requirements gathering, analysis, design, implementation, testing, and deployment. The requirements gathering activity is associated with the analysis activity where the requirements gathering activity plays the role of the previous activity and the analysis activity plays the role of the next activity. The analysis activity is associated with the design activity where the analysis activity plays the role of the previous activity and the design activity plays the role of the next activity. The design activity is associated with the implementation activity where the design activity plays the role of the previous activity and the implementation activity plays the role of the next activity. The design activity is associated with the implementation activity where the design activity plays the role of the previous activity and the implementation activity plays the role of the next activity. The implementation activity is associated with the testing activity where the implementation activity plays the role of the previous activity and the testing activity plays the role of the next activity. The testing activity is associated with the deployment activity where the testing activity plays the role of the previous activity and the deployment activity plays the role of the next activity.

    c. Nora and Phillip, who are workers, are on a project named Hawk. This project involves acquisition activities followed by implementation activities. Nora has 10 years of acquisition skills and 5 years of implementation skills. Phillip has 5 years of implementation skills. Nora and Phillip are associated with those activities that correspond to their skills. The project also has a plan, and Nora is the manager for the project.

6. Describe Figure 3-48: identify types, interfaces, undifferentiated classes, and implementation classes; and describe their attributes and operations. Update the diagram to reflect that a report is a type of documentation that may be viewed or printed, and is actually implemented as an artifact.

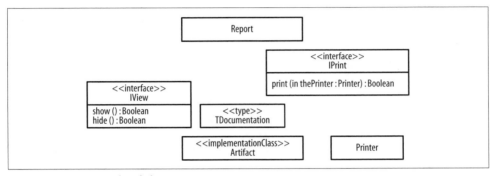

Figure 3-48. Report-related classes

7. Describe Figure 3-49: identify the subsystem and describe its specification elements and realization elements.

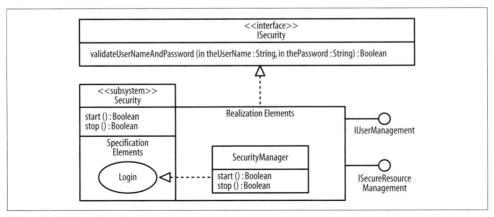

Figure 3-49. Security subsystem

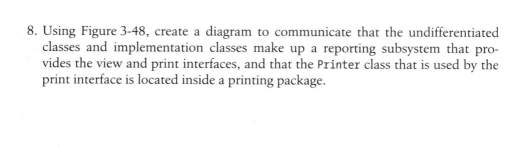

8. Using Figure 3-48, create a diagram to communicate that the undifferentiated classes and implementation classes make up a reporting subsystem that provides the view and print interfaces, and that the `Printer` class that is used by the print interface is located inside a printing package.

CHAPTER 4

Use-Case Diagrams

This chapter focuses on use-case diagrams, which depict the functionality of a system. First, I introduce use-case diagrams and how they are used. Next, I discuss actors and use cases. Finally, I go over various relationships relating to actors and use cases. Many details that were not fleshed out in Chapter 2 are more fully elaborated here, and throughout the chapter I include suggestions relating to use-case diagrams.

Use-case modeling is a specialized type of structural modeling concerned with modeling the functionality of a system. You usually apply use-case modeling during requirements activities to capture requirements that define what a system should do. Use-case modeling typically starts early in a project and continues throughout a system development process. It is usually done as a series of workshops between users and analysts of a system in which ideas can be explored and requirements may be fleshed out over time.

As a use-case driven process uses use cases to plan and perform iterations, it is important to understand how use cases are related to one another, including what use cases have in common, which use cases are options of other use cases, and which use cases are similar to each other. Given that every project has limited resources, you can use this information about use cases to determine how best to execute a project. Use cases that are common to two or more other use cases need only be implemented once, and then they can be reused. Use cases that are options of other use cases may be implemented at a later time, and use cases that are similar allow us to implement one use case that may be reused. An understanding of how use cases are related allows users and analysts to negotiate and reach agreement concerning the scope and requirements of a system.

A use-case diagram may be considered a "table of contents" for the functional requirements of a system. The details behind each element on the use case diagram may be captured in textual form or using other UML modeling techniques. All the use-case diagrams and their associated details for a specific system form the functional requirements of the system. However, the UML does not provide any explicit guidance on how to capture the textual details, but focuses more on the notation.

Actors

As discussed in Chapter 2, an *actor* is a user or external system with which a system being modeled interacts. For example, our project management system involves various types of users, including project managers, resource managers, human resources, and system administrators. These users are all actors.

Actors follow the type-instance dichotomy first discussed in Chapter 2 and applied to classes and objects in Chapter 3. You can use the UML to talk about classes of actors, as well as specific actors of a class. When speaking of a class of actors, it's customary to use the terms actor or *actor class*. Thus, while you might think of an actor as a specific thing, in the UML, an actor really represents a class of things. When speaking of a specific actor of a class, use the term *actor instance*.

An actor is external to a system, interacts with the system, may be a human user or another system, and has goals and responsibilities to satisfy in interacting with the system. Actors address the question of who and what interacts with a system. In the UML, an actor is shown as a "stick figure" icon, or as a class marked with the actor keyword and labeled with the name of the actor class.

Figure 4-1 shows various actors associated with the project management system:

A project manager
> Responsible for ensuring that a project delivers a quality product within specified time and cost, and within specified resource constraints

A resource manager
> Responsible for ensuring that trained and skilled human resources are available for projects

A human resource
> Responsible for ensuring that worker skills are maintained, and that quality work is completed for a project

A system administrator
> Responsible for ensuring that a project management system is available for a project

A backup system
> Responsible for housing backup data for a project management system

An actor instance is a specific user or system. For example, specific users of the project management system include Jonathan, Andy, Si, Phillip, Nora, and so forth. An actor instance is shown similar to an actor class, but is labeled with the actor instance name followed by a colon followed by the actor class name, all fully underlined. Both names are optional, and the colon is only present if the actor class name is specified. Actor instances address the question of who and what specifically interacts with a system.

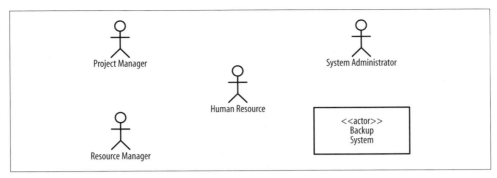

Figure 4-1. Actors

Figure 4-2 shows various actor instances of the actor classes in Figure 4-1, including Jonathan and Andy who are project managers, Si who is a human resource, Phillip who is a system administrator, Nora who is an unspecified type of actor instance, a backup system named BackupSys1.0, and other actor instances. Just as it's possible to have an actor of an unspecified type, such as Nora, it is possible to have actors such as HumanResource for which a type is specified, but not a name.

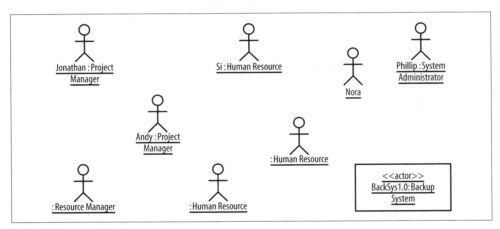

Figure 4-2. Actor instances

Because actors are external to a system and interact with that system, they define the boundary or scope of the system. For example, given the actors shown in Figure 4-1, we know exactly who and what will interact with the project management system. If we don't define our actors, we may fall into the trap of endlessly debating whether we have identified all the users of the system and all the other systems that interact with the system. Consequentially, because every functional requirement should be of interest to at least one user (otherwise, why would we build the system to provide the functionality?), without identifying actors, we have no way of knowing whether we have identified all the functional requirements of the system. An actor may also represent a resource owned by another project or purchased rather than built. For example, the backup system must be provided by another project, and it may be purchased from a vendor or built rather than purchased. Independent of how it is developed, we are interested in interacting with it as a resource.

Use Cases

As discussed in Chapter 2, a use case is a functional requirement that is described from the perspective of the users of a system. For example, functional requirements for the project management system include: security functionality (such as allowing users to log in and out of the system), inputting of data, processing of data, generation of reports, and so forth.

Use cases follow the type-instance dichotomy first discussed in Chapter 2 and applied to classes and object in Chapter 3. You can use the UML to talk about classes of use cases, and you can use the UML to talk about specific use cases of a class. When speaking of a class of use cases, it's customary to use the term use case or *use-case class*. Thus, while you might think of a use case as a specific thing, in the UML, a use case really represents a class of things. When speaking of a specific use case of a class, use the term *use-case instance*.

A use case defines a functional requirement that is described as a sequence of steps, which include actions performed by a system and interactions between the system and actors. Use cases address the question of how actors interact with a system, and describe the actions the system performs.

In the UML, a use case is shown as an ellipse and labeled with the name of the use-case class. Use cases may be enclosed by a rectangle that represents the boundary of the system that provides the functionality. Figure 4-3 shows various use cases associated with the project management system, including functionality to manage projects, manage resources, and administer the system.

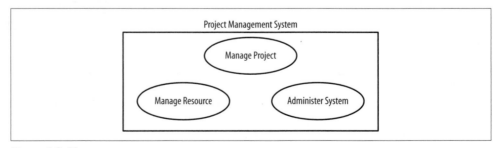

Figure 4-3. Use cases

A use-case instance, often called a *scenario*, is the performance of a specific sequence of actions and interactions. For example, a specific actor instance that uses security functionality to log in or out of the project management system represents a scenario. Other possible scenarios might include a user who enters data, a user who requests processing to be done on the data, or a user who requests that the system generate a report.

A use-case instance is shown similarly to a use case but labeled with the use-case instance name followed by a colon followed by the use-case name, all fully underlined. Both names are optional, and the colon is present only if the use-case class name is specified. Use-case instances address the questions of how actor instances specifically interact with a system and what specific actions the system performs in return. Use-case instances are not commonly shown on use-case diagrams but rather are simply discussed with users to better understand their requirements.

Because use cases are performed by a system, they define the functional requirements of the system. For example, given the use cases shown in Figure 4-3, we know generally what type of functionality must be provided by the project management system. Other use-case diagrams may refine and decompose these use cases. If we don't define our use cases, we may fall into the trap of endlessly debating whether we have identified all the functionality of the system.

Each use case is composed of one or more behavior sequences. A *behavior sequence* is a sequence of steps in which each step specifies an action or interaction. Each *action* specifies processing performed by the system. Each *interaction* specifies some communication between the system and one of the actors who participate in the use case. For example, a login use case may have the following behavior sequence:

1. The system provides a user interface to capture login information.
2. The user enters her username.
3. The user enters her password.
4. The system validates the username and password.
5. The system responds appropriately by allowing the user to continue, or by rejecting the user, depending on whether her username and password are valid.

Steps 1, 4, and 5 are actions that the system performs, and steps 2 and 3 are interactions between the system and user. It is fairly simple to see that step 4 is an action, but you may be wondering why steps 1 and 5 are actions rather than interactions, when the system is interacting with the user by presenting a user interface to the user or by responding appropriately with a message window or something similar. Steps 1 and 5 are actions rather than interactions because the system is simply taking action to show a user interface or a response message window that the user can easily choose to ignore. However, if this were not a human user but another system that would receive some communication to which it must reply, these would be interactions rather than actions. Quite often, trying to classify each step as either an action or interaction is not necessary; rather, it is more important to consider a use case as a dialog between actors and the system, to understand how actors interact with the system, and to understand what actions are the responsibility of the system.

Actions and interactions may also be repeated, conditional, or optional. For example, the `Manage Project` use case may have a behavior sequence for finding a project on which to work, and the following three succeeding behavior sequences:

- One for managing projects involving employees only
- One for managing projects involving consultants only
- One for managing projects involving both employees and consultants

An instance of the `Manage Project` use case involves actor instances and finding a project and managing it using one of the three available behavior sequences based upon the type of project selected. Behavior sequences, such as the one shown earlier for the login use case, are commonly captured in textual form, but may also be captured using behavioral modeling techniques, as discussed in Part III. However, the UML does not provide any explicit guidance on how to capture behavior sequences.

Because use cases result in some observable value to one or more actors, they must allow actors to achieve their goals. After all, each actor has goals in interacting with a system. Use cases don't represent actor goals, but instead represent functionality that enable actors to achieve their goals. For example, the use cases shown in Figure 4-3 enable the actors shown in Figure 4-1 to achieve their goals in the following ways:

- To ensure that a project delivers a quality product within the specified time, cost, and resource constraints, a project manager may use the `Manage Project` use case.
- To ensure that trained and skilled human resources are available for projects, a resource manager may use the `Manage Resource` use case.
- To ensure that a project management system is available for a project, a system administrator may use the `Administer System` use case, which may involve a backup system.

The project management system does not offer any functionality to enable human resources to achieve their goals. Note that such functionality is outside the scope of the system.

Communicate Associations

Figure 4-1 shows actors associated with the project management system and Figure 4-3 shows use cases associated with the project management system, but how are actors and use cases related? A specialized type of association, called a *communicate association*, addresses the question of how actors and use cases are related and which actors participate in or initiate use cases. (Associations are discussed in Chapter 3.)

As discussed in Chapter 2, a communicate association between an actor and a use case indicates that the actor uses the use case; that is, it indicates that the actor communicates with the system and participates in the use case. A use case may have associations with multiple actors, and an actor may have associations with multiple use cases. A communicate association is shown as a solid-line between an actor and a use case.

Figure 4-4 shows that a project manager participates in managing projects, a resource manager participates in managing resources, and a system administrator and backup system participates in administering the system.

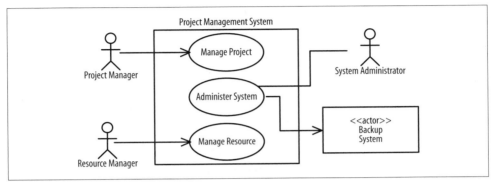

Figure 4-4. Actors and use cases

A navigation arrow on an association pointing toward a use case indicates that the actor initiates the interaction with the system. Figure 4-4 shows that a project manager initiates the interaction with the project management system to manage projects, and a resource manager initiates the interaction with the project management system to manage resources.

A navigation arrow on an association pointing toward an actor indicates that the system initiates the interaction with the actor. Figure 4-4 shows that the project management system initiates the interaction with the backup system to back up project management data.

Rather than use two arrows when either the system or the actor may initiate an interaction, navigation arrows on both ends of such an association are dropped. Figure 4-4 shows that either a system administrator or the system may initiate an interaction to administer the system. The system administrator might initiate an interaction with the system to back up the data, or, for example, the system might initiate an interaction with the system administrator informing the actor that system resources are low.

Be aware, however, that a lack of navigation arrows may simply result from a modeler choosing not to specify anything about the initiation of an interaction. Thus, with respect to Figure 4-4, you can't be absolutely certain that either actor can initiate a system administration interaction. It could be that the system administrator only can initiate the interaction, and the UML modeler simply chose not to specify initiation in this one case. It simply depends on the modeling guidelines the modeler is using.

Dependencies   USE CASES

A model may have many use cases, so how do we organize the use cases that define what a system should do? And how do we use this information about use cases to determine how best to execute a project while considering how use cases are related to one another, including what some use cases might have in common, and also taking into account use cases that are options of other use cases? Specialized types of dependencies, called include and extend dependencies, address these questions; dependencies are discussed in Chapter 3. The next few sections discuss these specialized types of dependencies.

Include Dependencies

Perhaps we wish to log the activities of project managers, resources managers, and system administrators as they interact with the project management system. Figure 4-5 elaborates on the use cases in Figure 4-4 to show that the activities of the project manager, resource managers, and system administrators are logged when they are performing the use cases shown in the diagram. Thus, logging activities are common to these three use cases. We can use an include dependency to address this type of situation by factoring out and reusing common behavior from multiple use cases.

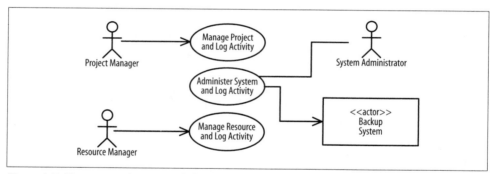

Figure 4-5. Use cases with common behavior

An *include dependency* from one use case (called the *base use case*) to another use case (called the *inclusion use case*) indicates that the base use case will include or call the inclusion use case. A use case may include multiple use cases, and it may be included in multiple use cases. An include dependency is shown as a dashed arrow from the base use case to the inclusion use case marked with the include keyword. The base use case is responsible for identifying where in its behavior sequence or at which step to include the inclusion use case. This identification is not done in the UML diagram, but rather in the textual description of the base use case.

Figure 4-6 refines Figure 4-5 using include dependencies. The Log Activity use case is common to the Manage Project, Manage Resource, and Administer System use cases, so it is factored out and included by these use cases.

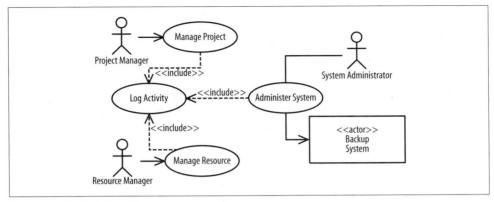

Figure 4-6. Include dependencies

You can use an include dependency when a use case may be common to multiple other use cases and is therefore factored out of the different use cases so that it may be reused. The Log Activity use case in Figure 4-6 is included in the Manage Project, Manage Resource, and Administer System use cases. Consequently, you must analyze and develop that use case before you develop the three use cases that depend on it.

Extend Dependencies

Projects are made of activities, and activities are made of tasks. Figure 4-7 elaborates the Manage Project use case in Figure 4-4, and shows that a project manager may manage projects by maintaining the project itself, its activities, or its tasks. Thus, maintaining the project, its activities, and its tasks are options of managing a project. You can use an extend dependency to address this situation by factoring out optional behavior from a use case.

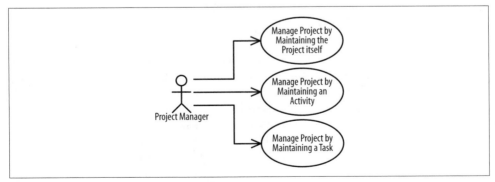

Figure 4-7. Use cases with optional behavior

An *extend dependency* from one use case (called the *extension use case*) to another use case (called the *base use case*) indicates that the extension use case will extend (or be inserted into) and augment the base use case. A use case may extend multiple use cases, and a use case may be extended by multiple use cases. An extend dependency is shown as a dashed arrow from the extension use case to the base use case marked with the extend keyword. The base use case is responsible for identifying at which steps in its behavior sequence the extending use cases may be inserted.

Figure 4-8 refines Figure 4-7 using extend dependencies. The Maintain Project, Maintain Activity, and Maintain Task use cases are options of the Manage Project use case, so Manage Project is factored out and extends those three use cases.

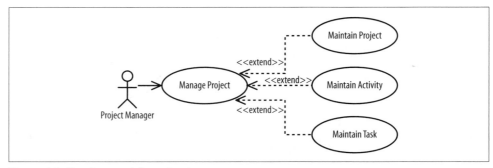

Figure 4-8. Simple extend dependencies

The location in a base use case at which another behavior sequence may be inserted is called an *extension point*. Extension points for a use case may be listed in a compartment labeled "Extension Points" where each extension point is shown inside the compartment with an extension-point name followed by a colon followed by a suitable description of the location of the extension point in the use case's behavior sequence. Locations may be described as being before, after, or in-the-place-of a step in the base use case's behavior sequence. For example, the Manage Project use case may have a behavior sequence for finding a project on which to work followed by an extension point named Project Selected followed by another behavior. The Project Selected extension point may be described as occurring after a project is found but before it is actually worked on.

An extend dependency is responsible for defining when an extension use case is inserted into the base use case by specifying a condition that must be satisfied for the insertion to occur. The condition may be shown following the extend keyword enclosed within square brackets followed by the extension point name enclosed in parentheses. For example, other use cases may be inserted into the Project Selected extension point just described for the Manage Project use case. Such behavior sequences may include reviewing and updating project information, or selecting a specific version of a project before managing the details of the project in the succeeding behavior sequences.

Figure 4-9 elaborates on the Administer System use case in Figure 4-4 using extend dependencies. It shows that a system administrator is offered two options—starting up the system or shutting down the system—at the extension point named Administration Functions, which is described as being available on the administration menu of the user interface. Figure 4-9 further shows the following:

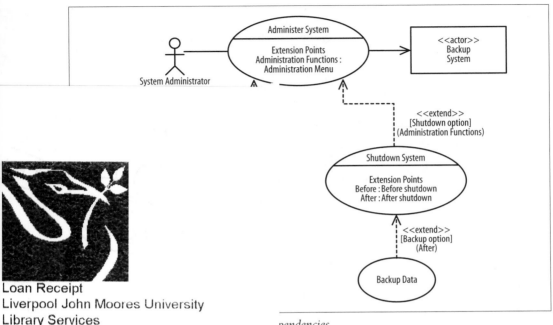

pendencies

available as an option at the Administration
Administer System use case. The Startup System
its named Before and After. The Before exten-
ing before the startup functionality is performed
tension point is described as occurring after the
ied by the system. These extension points are

is available as an option at the Before extension
use case. Before starting up the system, the sys-
ore data from the backup system to the project
ase that was previously archived.

bed for the After extension point of the Startup

s available as an option at the Administration
the Administer System use case. The Shutdown
System use case has two extension points, named Before and After. The Before extension point is described as occurring before the shutdown functionality is

performed by the system, and the After extension point is described as occurring after the shutdown functionality is performed by the system. These extension points are used as follows:

— The Backup Data use case is available as an option at the After extension point of the Shutdown System use case. After shutting down the system, the system administrator may back up data from the project management system's database to the backup system for later retrieval.

— There are no options described for the Before extension point of the Shutdown System use case.

The extension points just described allow us to insert behavior into the Startup System and Shutdown System use cases before or after they perform startup or shutdown processing for the project management system. The extend dependencies reference these extension points to indicate where use cases may be inserted inside one another, and also to indicate the conditions that must be satisfied for such an insertion to occur. Naturally, data is restored before the system is started up and data is backed up after the system is shut down.

Use an extend dependency when a use case is optional to another use case. Because the Maintain Project, Maintain Activity, and Maintain Task use cases extend the Manage Project use case, the Manage Project use case must be developed before the others; otherwise, the other use cases won't have a use case to extend. Likewise, the Administer System use case must be developed before the Startup System and Shutdown System use cases, Startup System must be developed before Restore Data, and Shutdown System must be developed before Backup Data. However, once Administer System is developed, Startup System and Shutdown System may be developed in parallel or concurrently, because they are not directly related.

Generalizations

Actors may be similar in how they use a system; for example, project managers, resource managers, and system administrators may log in and out of our project management system. Use cases may be similar in the functionality provided to users; for example, a project manager may publish a project's status in two ways: by generating a report to a printer or by generating a web site on a project web server.

Given that there may be similarities between actors and use cases, how do we organize the use cases that define what a system should do? And how do we use the information about similarities between actors and use cases to determine how best to execute a project? Specialized types of generalizations, called actor and use case generalizations, address these questions. Generalizations are introduced and discussed in Chapter 3. The next two sections discuss these specialized types of generalizations.

Actor Generalizations

Figure 4-10 shows that project managers, resource managers, and system administrators may log in and out of the project management system. Thus, logging in and out is common to these actors. Actor generalizations address such situations by factoring out and reusing similarities between actors.

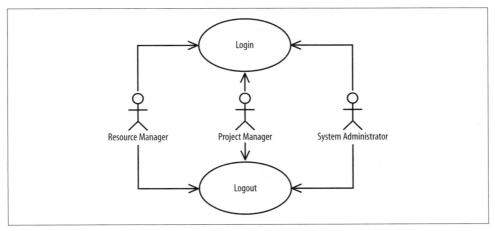

Figure 4-10. Similar actors

An *actor generalization* from a more specific, or *specialized*, actor to a more general, or *generalized*, actor indicates that instances of the more specific actor may be substituted for instances of the more general actor. An actor may specialize multiple actors, and an actor may be specialized by multiple actors. An actor generalization between actors is shown as a solid-line path from the more specific actor to the more general actor, with a large hollow triangle at the end of the path connected to the more general actor.

Figure 4-11 refines Figure 4-10 using actor generalizations between actors. A human resource initiates the Login and Logout use cases. Project managers, resource managers, and system administrators are human resources.

Use an actor generalization between actors when one actor is similar to another, but has specific interactions in which it participates or initiates. For example, any human resource may log in and out, but project managers, resources managers, and system administrators make more specialized use of the project management system. Because the Project Manager, Resource Manager, and System Administrator actors are specialized Human Resource actors, they benefit from the use cases in which the Human Resource actor is involved. Therefore, by developing the Login and Logout use cases, we provide the functionality described by those use cases for all the actors of our system.

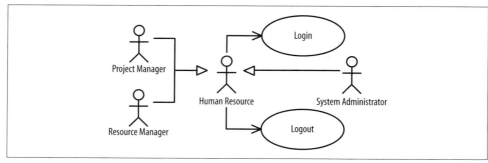

Figure 4-11. Actor generalizations

Use-Case Generalizations

Figure 4-12 shows that a project manager may publish a project's status in two ways: by generating a report to a printer or by generating a web site on a project web server. Thus, publishing a project's status and all the processing involved in collecting and preparing the data for publication is common to these use cases. You can use a use-case generalization to address this situation by factoring out and reusing similar behavior from multiple use cases.

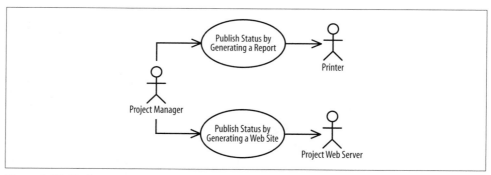

Figure 4-12. Similar use cases

A *use-case generalization* from a more specific, or *specialized*, use case to a more general, or *generalized*, use case indicates that the more specific use case receives or inherits the actors, behavior sequences, and extension points of the more general use case, and that instances of the more specific use case may be substituted for instances of the more general use case. The specific use case may include other actors, define new behavior sequences and extension points, and modify or specialize the behavior sequences it receives or inherits. A use case may specialize multiple use cases, and a use case may be specialized by multiple use cases. A use-case generalization between use cases is shown as a solid-line path from the more specific use case to the more general use case, with a large hollow triangle at the end of the path connected to the more general use case.

Figure 4-13 refines Figure 4-12 using use-case generalization between use cases. The Generate Report and Generate Website use cases receive the Project Manager actor, behavior sequences, and extension points of the Publish Status use case.

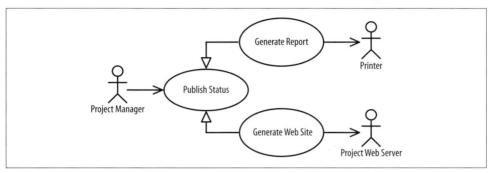

Figure 4-13. Use-case generalizations

You can use a use-case generalization between use cases when a more specific use case is similar to a more general use case but involves other actors or has specialized behavior. For example, a project manager may publish a project's status using a report or a web site, but a printer is involved only if a report is generated, and a project web server is involved only if a web site is generated. Because the Generate Report and Generate Website use cases specialize the Publish Status use case, Publish Status must be developed before the other use cases; otherwise, the other use cases won't have a use case to specialize.

It is important to understand the difference between include and extend dependencies and use-case generalization. An inclusion use case does not have knowledge of the base use case that includes it, an extension use case does not have knowledge of the base use case that it extends, and the Maintain Activity use case in Figure 4-8 has no knowledge of the use cases that it extends, so they can't involve the actors of the base use case in their behavior sequences. For example, the Log Activity use case in Figure 4-6 has no knowledge of the use cases that include it. However, a more specific use case receives or inherits the actors, behavior sequences, and extension points of its more general use case, so it can involve the actors of the more general use case in its behavior sequence. For example, the Generate Report use case in Figure 4-13 has knowledge of the Publish Status use case and may involve the Project Manager actor in its behavior sequence. An inclusion use case must be developed before its base use cases, an extension use case must be developed after its base use cases, and a more specific use case must be developed after its more general use cases.

Exercises

1. Describe Figure 4-14: identify actors and use cases, and describe the relationships among actors and use cases.

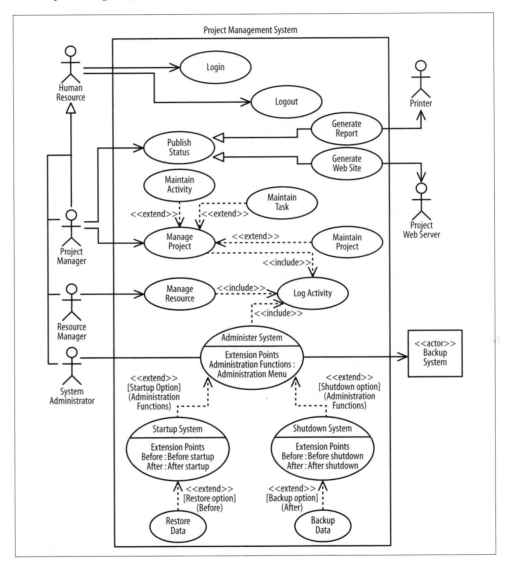

Figure 4-14. Use-case diagram for the project management system

2. Update the diagram shown in Figure 4-14 stepwise to show the following details. After each step, check your answers against the solutions shown in Appendix B:

a. A human resource may manage his professional development plan. When managing his professional development plan, the human resource may manage his profile. In managing his professional development plan, he will have access to a training schedule provided by a training database, and all the information pertaining to his professional development plan will be stored in a professional development plan database. Both databases are not part of the project management system.

b. When a resource manager manages resources, she will have access to resource functions that are provided on a resource menu. One option is to manage a resource's profile. This is the same functionality used by human resources to manage their profiles.

c. A project manager or system administrator, acting as an email user, may send email using an email system that is not constructed as part of the development effort (it may have been purchased). When sending email, the manager may select a secure option wherein his whole interaction with the system is secured using a purchased encryption engine. Note that this is not simply encrypting the sent email message, but encrypting the entire interaction as the email is composed and sent.

d. An email system may be used to receive email messages. When a message is received, the email user is informed. Likewise, an email user may query the system to check whether new messages have arrived, depending on how often her system is set up to check for new messages.

e. When sending or receiving email, the system logs the transaction. This functionality for logging transactions may be used by other use cases in the future.

3. Given Figure 4-14 and the solution to question 2, describe the general order in which the use cases shown in the resulting diagram must be developed; that is, what use cases must be developed before other use cases (independent of users prioritizing the use cases)?

CHAPTER 5

Component and Deployment Diagrams

This chapter focuses on component and deployment diagrams, which depict the implementation and environment of a system, respectively. First, I introduce component and deployment diagrams and how they are used. Next, I discuss components and nodes, which are elements depicted on those diagrams. Finally, I discuss various relationships relating to components and nodes. Many details of our project management system that were not fleshed out in Chapter 2 are more fully elaborated here, and throughout the chapter, I include suggestions relating to component and deployment diagrams.

Component modeling is a specialized type of structural modeling concerned with modeling the implementation of a system. Using the UML, you can communicate the implementation of a system using component diagrams. You usually apply component modeling during design activities to determine how implementation activities will build the system; that is, to determine the elements of the system on which implementation activities will focus. Component modeling typically starts after the design of the system is fairly complete, as determined by your system development process.

Deployment modeling is a specialized type of structural modeling concerned with modeling the implementation environment of a system. In contrast to modeling the components of a system, a deployment model shows you the external resources that those components require. You typically apply deployment modeling during design activities to determine how deployment activities will make the system available to its users; that is, to determine the elements of the system on which deployment activities will focus. Like component modeling, deployment modeling usually starts after the design of the system is fairly complete, as determined by your system development process.

Components

As mentioned in Chapter 2, a component is a part of the system that exists when the system is executing. For example, the project management system may be decomposed into the following components:

A user interface component
> Responsible for providing a user interface through which users may interact with the system

A business-processing component
> Responsible for implementing business functionality, including all the project management functionality provided by the project management system

A data component
> For implementing data storage functionality

A security component
> Provides various forms of security functionality to the business-processing and data components, including user authentication and verifying user privileges when accessing data

Components follow the type-instance dichotomy first discussed in Chapter 2 and applied to classes and objects in Chapter 3. You can use the UML to talk about classes of components as well as specific components of a class. When speaking of a class of components, it's customary to use the terms component or *component class*. Thus, while you might think of a component as a specific thing, in the UML, a component really represents a class of things. When speaking of a specific component of a class, use the term *component instance*.

A component exists during execution time and requires a resource on which to execute, which I talk about in the next section, "Nodes." In the UML, a component is shown as a rectangle with two small rectangles protruding from its side. The rectangle is labeled with the name of the component class.

Figure 5-1 shows various components associated with the project management system, including user interface, business-processing, data, and security components.

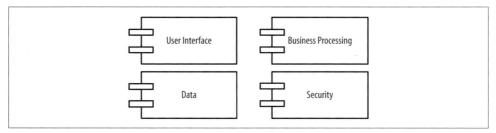

Figure 5-1. Components of the project management system

A component instance is a specific component. For example, specific components of the project management system include:

A web user interface component instance
> Allows users to access the project management system via the Web

A client/server user interface component instance
> Allows users to access the project management system in a client/server environment

A local data component instance
> Stores project management data for a specific user or group of users

An enterprise data component instance
> Stores project management data for a complete organization

A component instance is shown similar to a component class, but is labeled with the component instance name followed by a colon followed by the component class name, with all parts of the name fully underlined. Both names are optional, and the colon is present only if the component class name is specified.

Figure 5-2 shows various component instances of the component classes in Figure 5-1, including two user interface component instances, named Web and Client Server, two data component instances, named Local Data and Enterprise Data, a nameless business processing component instance, and a nameless security component instance.

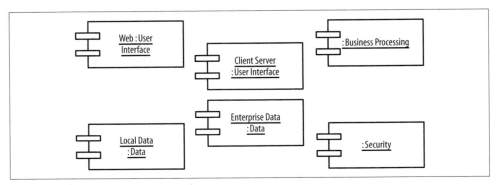

Figure 5-2. Component instances in the project management system

Nodes

A *node* is a resource that is available during execution time. (Nodes were mentioned in Chapter 2.) Traditionally, nodes refer to computers on a network, but in the UML a node may be a computer, printer, server, Internet, or any other kind of resource available to components. For example, the project management system may be deployed on the following nodes:

A desktop client
> On which the user interface component executes

A printer
> Which the project management system uses to print reports

A business-processing server
> On which the business-processing component executes

A database server
> On which the data component executes and where project-related information is stored

Nodes follow the type-instance dichotomy first discussed in Chapter 2 and applied to classes and objects in Chapter 3. You can use the UML to talk about classes of nodes, as well as specific nodes of a class. When speaking of a class of nodes, it's customary to use the terms node or *node class*. Thus, while you might think of a node as a specific thing, in the UML, a node really represents a class of nodes. When speaking of a specific component of a class, use the term *node instance*.

A node is available during execution time and is a resource on which components may execute. In the UML, a node is shown as a three-dimensional rectangle labeled with the node's name.

Figure 5-3 shows various nodes associated with the project management system, including a desktop client, business-processing server, database server, and printer node.

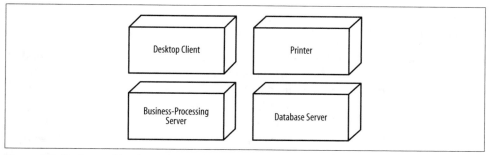

Figure 5-3. Nodes used by the project management system

A node instance is a specific node. For example, specific nodes used by the project management system include:

A desktop client node instance
　　Used by Jonathan to access the project management system

A desktop client node instance
　　Used by Andy to access the project management system

A group business-processing server node instance
　　Used by a group of users to manage projects

An enterprise business-processing server node instance
　　Used by a complete organization to manage projects

A node instance is shown similarly to a node class but labeled with the node instance name followed by a colon followed by the node class name, all fully underlined. Both names are optional, and the colon is present only if the node class name is specified.

Figure 5-4 shows various node instances of the node classes in Figure 5-3, including two desktop client node instances, named Jonathan's Computer and Andy's Computer, two business-processing node instances, named Group Server and Enterprise Server, a printer node instance, named Group Printer, and a database server node instance.

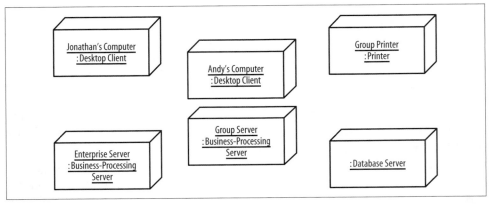

Figure 5-4. Node instances

Dependencies

Figure 5-1 shows components associated with the project management system, and Figure 5-3 shows nodes associated with the project management system, but how are components related to undifferentiated and differentiated classes, packages, subsystems, and to other components and nodes? Specialized types of dependencies—called reside, use, and deploy dependencies—address these questions. The next few sections in this chapter discuss these specialized types of dependencies. Dependences in general are discussed in Chapter 3.

Reside Dependencies

A *reside* dependency from a component to any UML element indicates that the component is a client of the element, which is itself considered a supplier, and that the element resides in the component. The element may be an undifferentiated or differentiated class, package, or subsystem. An element may reside in any number of components, and a component may have any number of elements that reside in it.

A reside dependency is shown as a dashed arrow from a client component to a supplier element marked with the reside keyword. Figure 5-5 shows that the User Interface and Utility packages reside in the User Interface component. Because the User Interface package depends on the Utility package, the User Interface and Utility packages must reside in the same component; otherwise, the User Interface package would not be able to use the Utility package.

Figure 5-6 shows that the Business Processing subsystem and Utility package reside in the Business Processing component. Because the Business Processing subsystem provides the IBusiness Processing interface, the Business Processing component also provides the interface. Again, because the Business Processing subsystem depends on the Utility package, the Business Processing subsystem and Utility

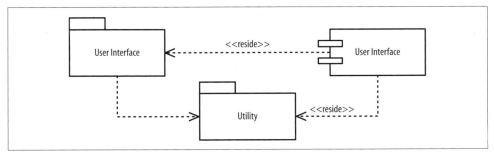

Figure 5-5. Reside dependencies for packages

package must reside in the same component; otherwise, the Business Processing subsystem would not be able to use the Utility package. Remember, it's perfectly fine for an element to reside in more than one component. For example, the Utility package resides in both the User Interface and Business Processing components, and, as you will soon see, in the Data component.

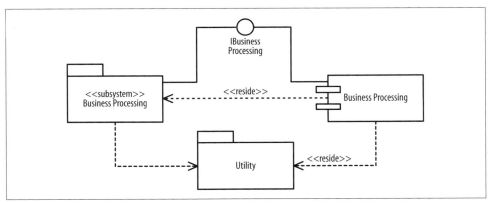

Figure 5-6. Reside dependencies for subsystems

Alternatively, an element that resides inside a component may be shown nested inside the component. Figure 5-7 shows that the Data subsystem and Utility package reside in the Data component. The Data subsystem is drawn inside the Data component, while the reside dependency to Utility is still drawn in the same manner as in Figures 5-5 and 5-6.

Notice that the Utility package resides in all the components in Figures 5-5, 5-6, and 5-7, because each component described in those figures has a package that uses the Utility package. Details of the Utility package are discussed in Chapter 3.

Use Dependencies

A *use* dependency from a client component to a supplier component indicates that the client component uses or depends on the supplier component. A use dependency

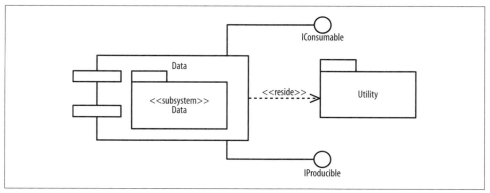

Figure 5-7. Reside dependencies using nesting

from a client component to a supplier component's interface indicates that the client component uses or depends on the interface provided by the supplier component. A use dependency is shown as a dashed arrow from a client component to a supplier component or a supplier component's interface. The dependency may be marked with the use keyword; however, the keyword is often omitted because this is the default, and the meaning is evident from how the dependency is used.

Figure 5-8 shows how the various components of the project management system are related:

The User Interface *component*
> Uses the Security component and the IBusiness Processing interface provided by the Business Processing component

The Business Processing *component*
> Uses the Security component and the IProducible and IConsumable interfaces provided by the Data component

The Data *component*
> Uses the Security component

Deploy Dependencies

A *deploy* dependency from a client component to a supplier node indicates that the client component is deployed on the supplier node.

A deploy dependency is shown as a dashed arrow from a client component to a supplier node marked with the deploy keyword. Figure 5-9 shows that the User Interface component is deployed on the Desktop Client node.

Figure 5-10 shows that the Business Processing component is deployed on the Business-Processing Server node.

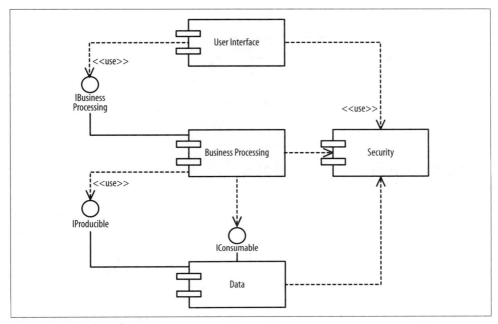

Figure 5-8. Use dependencies

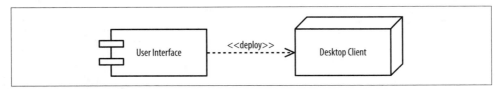

Figure 5-9. Deploy dependencies

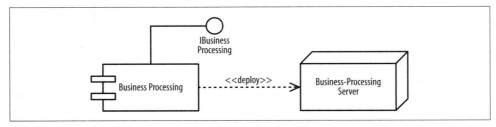

Figure 5-10. Deploy dependencies for a subsystem

Alternatively, a component that is deployed on a node may be shown nested inside the node. Figure 5-11 shows that the Data component is deployed on the Database Server node.

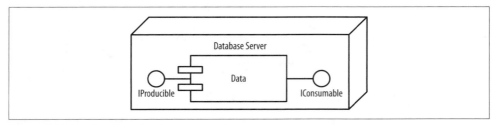

Figure 5-11. Deploy dependencies using nesting

Communication Associations

Figure 5-3 shows nodes associated with the project management system, but how are those nodes related? A specialized type of association, called a communication association, addresses the question of how nodes are related. (Associations are discussed in Chapter 3.)

A communication association between nodes indicates a communication path between the nodes that allows components on the nodes to communicate with one another. A communication association is shown as a solid-line between nodes. Figure 5-12 shows that the Business-Processing Server has a communication association with the Desktop Client, Printer, and Database Server nodes.

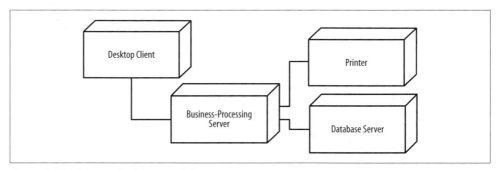

Figure 5-12. Communication associations

Figure 5-13 combines Figure 5-8 and Figure 5-12 to show how components are related to nodes. Notice that if two components are related and reside on different nodes, the nodes must have a communication association between them to allow the components to communicate; otherwise, the components are not able to communicate and be related to one another. For example, if the communication association between the Desktop Client and Business-Processing Server nodes was removed, the User Interface component could not be related to the IBusiness Processing interface and Security component. If the communication association between the Business-Processing Server and Database Server nodes was removed, the Data component could not be related to the Security component, and the Business Processing component could not be related to the IProducible and IConsumable interfaces.

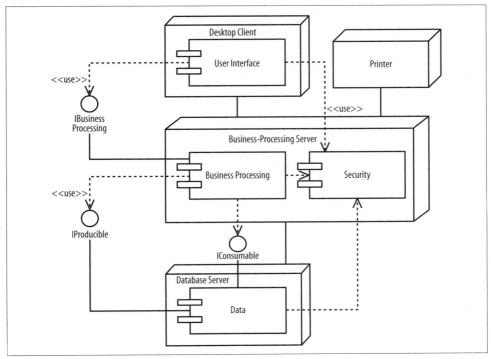

Figure 5-13. Communication associations

Exercises

1. Describe Figure 5-14: identify components and nodes, and describe the relationships among components and nodes.

2. Describe Figure 5-15: identify the various elements and their relationships.

   Update the diagram stepwise to show the following details. After each step, check your answers against the solutions shown in Appendix B:

   a. The User Interface package uses the IView and IPrint interfaces provided by the Reporting subsystem.

   b. The User Interface and Utility packages resides in a User Interface component.

   c. The Reporting subsystem and Utility package reside in a Reporting component.

   d. The User Interface component is deployed on a Desktop Client node.

   e. The Reporting component is deployed on a Report Server node.

   f. The Desktop Client node is connected to the Report Server node, and the Report Server node is connected to a High-speed Printer node.

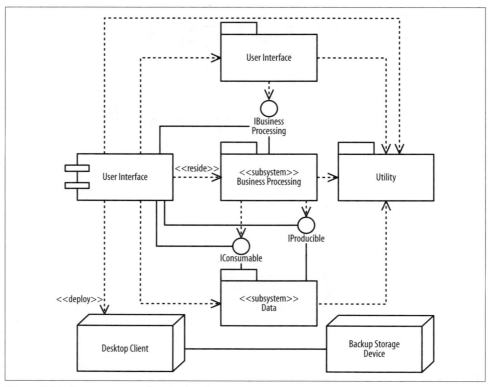

Figure 5-14. Components and nodes for the project management system

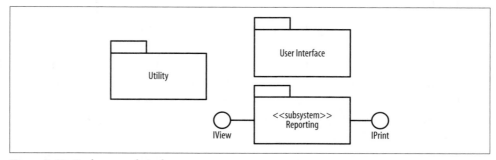

Figure 5-15. Packages and a subsystem

PART III

Behavioral Modeling

CHAPTER 6

Sequence and Collaboration Diagrams

This chapter focuses on sequence and collaboration diagrams. *Sequence diagrams* depict the dynamic behavior of elements that make up a system as they interact over time. *Collaboration diagrams* depict the behavior of elements as they interact over time *and* are related in space. As an architecture-centric process focuses on the architecture of a system across iterations, it is important to understand how elements that make up a system interact and collaborate with one another to provide the functionality of the system. We can use this information to determine how best to develop a system. This allows architects, designers, and developers to ensure that the system, when implemented, satisfies its requirements.

There is some redundancy between sequence and collaboration diagrams in that they both show how elements interact over time. However, the emphasis of each diagram is somewhat different. Sequence diagrams allow you to focus more on the time line in which events occur, while collaboration diagrams make it easier to show relationships between objects.

First, I introduce sequence and collaboration diagrams and how they are used. Next, I discuss roles that classes, objects, associations, and links play in an interaction and collaboration. Then, I go over the communications they exchange when playing these roles. Finally, I discuss how to capture interactions and collaborations. Many details that were not fleshed out in Chapter 2 are more fully elaborated here, and throughout the chapter, I include suggestions relating to sequence and collaboration diagrams.

Interaction modeling is a specialized type of behavioral modeling concerned with modeling how elements interact over time. Collaboration modeling is a specialized type of behavioral modeling concerned with modeling how elements relate to each other as they interact over time. Using the UML, you can communicate how elements interact over time and how they are related using collaboration diagrams. You usually apply interaction and collaboration modeling during analysis and design

sequence

activities to understand the requirements and determine how a system will satisfy its requirements. Interaction and collaboration modeling usually start after requirements have matured enough, as determined by your system development process, and continue in parallel with class and object modeling (Chapter 3) throughout a system development process.

Roles

As discussed in Chapter 2, the object-oriented paradigm views the world as a collection of unique elements (objects, classes, subsystems, and so forth), often referred to as a *society of objects*, which communicate with one another. Communication from a sender element to a receiver element is used to convey information or request processing. The word "objects" is used in the phrase "society of objects" rather than "classes," "subsystems," or any other word, because objects are the most fundamental, or primitive, parts of the object-oriented paradigm. It is also common to use the phrase "society of elements."

For example, Figure 6-1, a use-case diagram, shows that a project manager may request that the project management system generate a project-status report that is sent to a printer. The Generate Project-Status Report use case involves a Project Manager actor who initiates the generation of the report and a Printer actor through which the report is printed, as discussed in Chapter 4.

Figure 6-1. Generating a project-status report

The Generate Project-Status Report use case may have the following description:

1. The project manager enters the name of the project of interest.
2. The system generates the report.
3. The system sends the report to the printer.
4. The printer prints the report.

Notice how all the actors and the system are involved in this description. The description indicates that the system will generate the report, but it does not indicate how.

To provide the functionality for the report, a society of objects must work together in much the same way the classes in Figure 6-2 do. Figure 6-2 shows that an organization may execute any number of projects. An object of the Organization class may contain zero or more objects of the Project class, and each object of the Project class must be contained by no more than one object of the Organization class, as discussed in Chapter 3. Therefore, these classes and others could be used to form a society of objects that work together to provide the functionality of the Generate Project-Status Report use case.

Figure 6-2. Organizations and projects

As the classes in Figure 6-2 may interact and collaborate with other classes to provide the functionality in Figure 6-1, each class or association may play a role within that interaction and collaboration. A *role* is a placeholder for an object or link to play in an interaction and collaboration. Elements that play such roles are known as *participating elements*. For example, the participating elements in the Generate Project-Status Report use case may play the following roles:

Initiator
    Played by a project manager; responsible for initiating the use case

Output device
    Played by a printer; responsible for printing the generated report

Project organization
    Played by an object of the Organization class; responsible for containing the project that is the subject of the report

Project reference
    Played by a link of the Execute association; responsible for referring to the project that is the subject of the report

Project
    Played by an object of the Project class; subject of the report

To generate the report in an interaction and collaboration, I can use an object of the Project class to access information about the project directly, or I can use a link of the Execute association as a means to access an object of the Project class. Because I want to demonstrate how to use classes and objects as well as associations and links in interactions and collaborations, I will focus on the Organization class and Execute association rather than the Organization class and Project class.

In the UML, the use of an interaction and collaboration is depicted as a dashed ellipse containing the name of the interaction and collaboration. The interaction and collaboration may be attached to the use case that it realizes using a realization relationship, as discussed in Chapter 3. Figure 6-3, a use-case diagram, shows that the Generate Project-Status Report interaction and collaboration realizes the Generate Project-Status Report use case. It is quite common to use the same name for the interaction and collaboration as the use case it realizes.

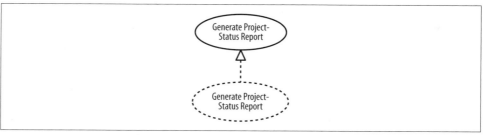

Figure 6-3. Interaction and collaboration realizing a use case

The Generate Project-Status Report interaction and collaboration may have the following description using the initiator, output device, project organization, and project reference roles just described:

1. The initiator role enters the name of the project for which the report is to be generated and submits this information to the system.

2. The request to generate the project-status report is received by a handler element that is responsible for managing the overall generation of the report.

3. The handler element creates a report element that is an abstraction of the generated report. That is, the report element represents within the system the report that is generated.

4. The handler element retrieves information about the organization from the project organization role and about the project using the project reference role, formats the information, and outputs the formatted information to the report element.

5. If the project is a newly created or unpopulated project that does not have any information (that is, no workers, units of work, and no work products are yet defined), the handler element requests that the project organization element indicates this on the report element.

6. If the project does have some information, the handler element requests that the project organization element continue generating information for the report element.

   a. The project organization role retrieves all the workers of the project and requests that the project output the contact information for each worker using the project reference role. The project organization role does not do any formatting of this output.

   b. For each worker, the project organization role retrieves the worker's units of work and work products using the project reference role, formats this information, and outputs the formatted information to the report element. The project organization role does all the formatting of this output.

7. The handler element prints the report element.

8. The handler element destroys the report element. That is, it destroys the element that represents within the system the report that is generated.

9. The output device role prints the report received from the system.

Notice how all the roles and other elements are involved in this description. The description elaborates on the Generate Project-Status Report use case and indicates how the system will generate the report:

- Step 1 of the use case description is equivalent to step 1 of the interaction and collaboration description.

- Steps 2 and 3 of the use case description are elaborated into steps 2 through 8 of the interaction and collaboration description.

- Step 4 of the use case description is equivalent to step 9 of the interaction and collaboration description.

The roles in the Generate Project-Status Report interaction and collaboration can be classified as class roles and association roles.

Classes and Objects

A *class role* defines a specific use of an object of a class; objects of the class are said to conform to the class role. For example, a project manager plays the role of an initiator, a printer plays the role of an output device, and an organization plays the role of an organization that contains the project that is the subject of a project-status report.

To show that objects of a class conform to a class role, a dashed line is drawn from the interaction and collaboration symbol to the class and labeled with the role objects of the class play in the interaction and collaboration. For example, Figure 6-4, a diagram that uses elements from a use-case diagram and a class diagram, combines Figures 6-1 through 6-3 to show the initiator, outputDevice, and projectOrganization class roles.

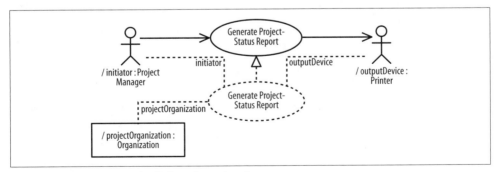

Figure 6-4. Interaction and collaboration using classes

In addition, Figure 6-4 demonstrates two methods for identifying a role. One method involves labeling the dashed line to indicate that objects of a class conform to a role. You may also show a class using the notation for classes as defined in Chapter 3, but with the class name preceded by a forward slash followed by the name of the role followed by a colon—for example, /projectOrganization:Organization. The forward slash indicates that the name to follow, projectOrganization, is a rolename. That is followed by a colon and, finally, the class name, which in this case is Organization. Usually, you will want to use just one of these methods consistently.

To show that a specific object of a class conforms to a class role, a dashed line is drawn from the interaction and collaboration symbol to the object and labeled with the role the specific object of the class plays in the interaction and collaboration. As with a class, rather than label the dashed line, you may show an object using the notation for objects as defined in Chapter 3, but the object name is followed by a forward slash followed by the name of the role followed by a colon followed by the class name, all fully underlined.

For example, Figure 6-5, which is a diagram that uses the elements from a use-case diagram and an object diagram, shows that Andy plays the role of an initiator, Andy's printer plays the role of an output device, and Andy's organization plays the role of an organization that contains the project that is the subject of the report.

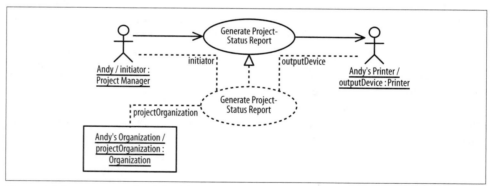

Figure 6-5. Interaction and collaboration using objects

Associations and Links

An *association role* defines a specific use of a link of an association. Links of the association are said to conform to the association role. For example, an execute relationship plays the role of a reference to the project that is the subject of a project-status report.

To show that links of an association conform to an association role, a dashed line is drawn from the interaction and collaboration symbol to the association and labeled with the role links of the association play in the interaction and collaboration. Also, rather than label the dashed line, you may show the association using notation similar to that used for classes in Figure 6-4: the association name is preceded by a forward slash followed by the name of the role followed by a colon.

For example, Figure 6-6 updates Figure 6-4 and shows the `projectReference` association role.

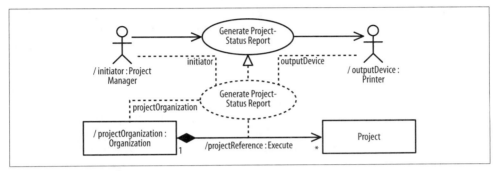

Figure 6-6. Interaction and collaboration using associations

To show that a specific link of an association conforms to an association role, a dashed line is drawn from the interaction and collaboration symbol to the link and labeled with the role the specific link of the association plays in the interaction and collaboration. Also, rather than label the dashed line, you may show the link using notation similar to that used for objects in Figure 6-5: the association name is preceded by a forward slash followed by the role followed by a colon. Recall from Chapter 3 that a link may have its association name shown near the path fully underlined, but links do not have instance names.

For example, Figure 6-7 updates Figure 6-5 and shows the `projectReference` link role.

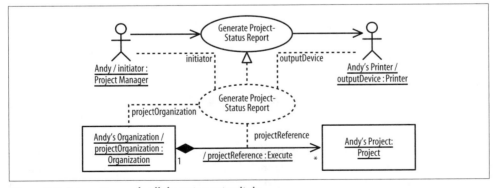

Figure 6-7. Interaction and collaboration using links

Messages and Stimuli

As discussed in Chapter 2, communication from a sender object to a receiver object via a link is called a *stimulus*, and communication from a sender class to a receiver class via an association is called a *message*. A stimulus is an instance of a message much the way an object is an instance of a class and a link is an instance of an association. For example, the objects in Figure 6-5 and Figure 6-7 would exchange stimuli and the classes in Figure 6-4 and Figure 6-6 would exchange messages. The sender object (or class) is known as the *client*, and the receiver object (or class) is known as the *supplier*.

Within an interaction and collaboration, messages are exchanged between a sender class role and a receiver class role via an association role, and stimuli are exchanged between a sender object playing a class role and a receiver object playing a class role via a link playing an association role. For example, Figure 6-4 and Figure 6-6 show that class roles would exchange messages via association roles, and Figure 6-5 and Figure 6-7 show that objects playing class roles would exchange stimuli via links playing association roles. As discussed in Chapter 2, in the object-oriented paradigm, communication from a sender to a receiver is used to convey information or request processing.

Interactions and Collaborations

Formally, a collection of classes, their messages, and their associations is known as a *collaboration*. A collection of specific objects playing the roles of the classes, their stimuli, and their specific links playing the roles of the associations, is known as a *collaboration instance*. A collection of messages is known as an *interaction* and a collection of stimuli is known as an *interaction instance*. An interaction is said to occur within the context of a collaboration because an interaction is a subset of the contents of a collaboration; and an interaction instance is said to occur within the context of a collaboration instance because an interaction instance is a subset of the contents of a collaboration instance.

You may show an interaction using one of two forms:

Generic-form interaction
> Shows two or more possible sequences of message or stimuli exchanges using repetition and conditionality.

> *Repetition*
>> Involves repeating a set of messages or stimuli—for example, repeating the set of messages or stimuli in steps 6a and 6b of the interaction and collaboration description to generate the project-status report.

Conditionality

Involves communicating one set of messages or stimuli rather than another set of messages or stimuli—for example, conditionally performing step 5 or 6 of the interaction and collaboration description to generate the project-status report.

Instance-form interaction

Shows one actual sequence of message or stimuli exchanges without any repetition or conditionality. For example, generating a specific project-status report that contains exactly three workers, each with two units of work and one work product. Rather than showing repetition and conditionality as in a generic-form interaction, instance-form interactions show the actual set of messages or stimuli that are repeated and the set of messages or stimuli that are communicated for specific conditions.

You may show a collaboration using one of two levels:

Specification-level collaboration

Shows class roles, association roles, and their messages. For example, you might use class roles, association roles, and their messages to communicate a generic-form or instance-form interaction.

Instance-level Collaboration

Shows specific objects, links, and their stimuli. For example, you might use objects, links, and their stimuli to communicate a generic-form or instance-form interaction.

In the UML, sequence and collaboration diagrams, rather than textual descriptions, are used to capture the details of interactions, collaborations, interaction instances, and collaboration instances. The interaction forms and collaboration levels just described make the UML very expressive.

Sequence Diagrams

A sequence diagram shows elements as they interact over time, showing an interaction or interaction instance. Sequence diagrams are organized along two axes: the horizontal axis shows the elements that are involved in the interaction, and the vertical axis represents time proceeding down the page. The elements on the horizontal axis may appear in any order.

Elements

Sequence diagrams are made up of a number of elements, including class roles, specific objects, lifelines, and activations. All of these are described in the following subsections.

Class roles

In a sequence diagram, a class role is shown using the notation for a class as defined in Chapter 3, but the class name is preceded by a forward slash followed by the name of the role that objects must conform to in order to participate within the role, followed by a colon. Other classes may also be shown as necessary, using the notation for classes as defined in Chapter 3.

Class roles and other classes are used for specification-level collaborations communicated using sequence diagrams. Figure 6-8 shows the projectOrganization class role as well as the Project and Report classes.

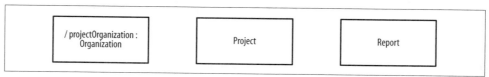

Figure 6-8. A class role and two classes

Specific objects

In a sequence diagram, a specific object of a class conforming to a class role is shown using the notation for objects as defined in Chapter 3, but the object name is followed by a forward slash followed by the name of the role followed by a colon followed by the class name, all fully underlined. Other objects may also be shown as necessary using the notation for objects, as defined in Chapter 3.

Specific objects conforming to class roles and other objects are used for instance-level collaborations communicated using sequence diagrams. Figure 6-9 shows that Andy's organization plays the role of an organization that contains a project that is the subject of the report. Figure 6-9 also shows anonymous Project and Report objects.

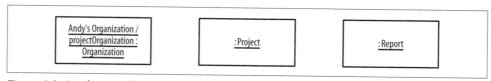

Figure 6-9. An object conforming to a class role

Lifelines

A *lifeline*, shown as a vertical dashed line from an element, represents the existence of the element over time. Figure 6-10 shows lifelines for the class role (projectOrganization) and classes (Project and Report) in Figure 6-8. Lifelines may also be shown for the objects in Figure 6-9.

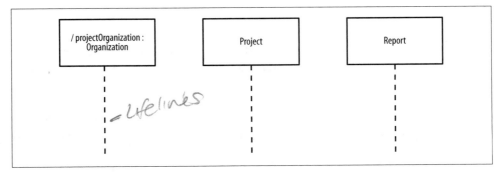

Figure 6-10. Lifelines

Activations

An optional *activation*, shown as a tall, thin rectangle on a lifeline, represents the period during which an element is performing an operation. The top of the rectangle is aligned with the initiation time, and the bottom is aligned with the completion time. Figure 6-11 shows activations for the class roles in Figure 6-8, where all the elements are simultaneously performing operations. Activations may also be shown for the objects in Figure 6-9.

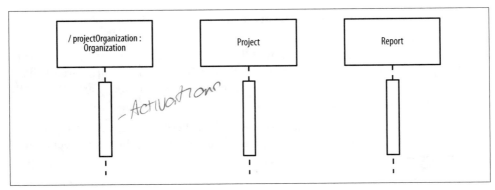

Figure 6-11. Activations

Communication

In a sequence diagram, a communication, message, or stimulus is shown as a horizontal solid arrow from the lifeline or activation of a sender to the lifeline or activation of a receiver. In the UML, communication is described using the following UML syntax:

```
[guard] *[iteration] sequence_number : return_variable := operation_name
    (argument_list)
```

in which:

guard

Is optional and indicates a condition that must be satisfied for the communication to be sent or occur. The square brackets are removed when no guard is specified.

iteration

Is optional and indicates the number of times the communication is sent or occurs. The asterisk and square brackets are removed when no iteration is specified.

sequence_number

Is an optional integer that indicates the order of the communication. The succeeding colon is removed when no sequence number is specified. Because the vertical axis represents time proceeding down the page on a sequence diagram, a sequence number is optional.

return_variable

Is optional and indicates a name for the value returned by the operation. If you choose not to show a return variable, or the operation does not return a value, you should also omit the succeeding colon and equal sign.

operation_name

Is the name of the operation to be invoked.

argument_list

Is optional and is a comma-separated list that indicates the arguments passed to the operation. Each parameter may be an explicit value or a return variable from a preceding communication. If an operation does not require any arguments, the parentheses are left empty.

Figure 6-12 shows the communication occurring between the GenerateProject-StatusReportHandler class (which is responsible for managing the overall generation of the project status report) and the projectOrganization class role.

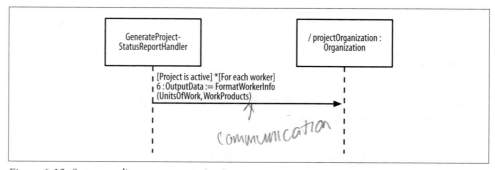

Figure 6-12. Sequence diagram communications

Let's take a step-wise look at how the communication notation used in Figure 6-12 is built. To begin with, the communication invokes a `FormatWorkerInfo` operation that formats a worker's information:

```
FormatWorkerInfo
```

This operation requires a worker's units of work and work products, so we can update the communication to the following:

```
FormatWorkerInfo (UnitsOfWork, WorkProducts)
```

The operation also returns some output data as a string of formatted text, so we update the communication to reflect this:

```
OutputData := FormatWorkerInfo (UnitsOfWork, WorkProducts)
```

In our earlier description of this interaction and collaboration, this operation occurs as the sixth communication in an overall sequence of communications:

```
6 : OutputData := FormatWorkerInfo (UnitsOfWork, WorkProducts)
```

A project may involve more than one worker, thus the operation is to occur once for each worker: We indicate this using the notation for repetition:

```
*[For each worker] 6 : OutputData := FormatWorkerInfo (UnitsOfWork, WorkProducts)
```

Finally, this operation is to occur only if a project is active, and we indicate this using guard notation:

```
[Project is active] *[For each worker] 6 : OutputData := FormatWorkerInfo
(UnitsOfWork, WorkProducts)
```

 The UML also allows you to show communication using pseudocode or another language. For example, you can use the syntax of Java, C++, C#, or some other programming language. A communication may also be described in the left margin of the sequence diagram.

Reflexive communication

Similar to a reflexive association or link, as discussed in Chapter 3, an element may communicate with itself where a communication is sent from the element to itself. In the UML, a reflexive communication is shown as a horizontal solid arrow from the lifeline or activation of an element that loops back to the same lifeline or activation of the element.

Figure 6-13 shows a reflexive communication for step 6 of the `Generate Project-Status Report` interaction and collaboration description where the `GenerateProject-StatusReportHandler` class formats the organization and project information.

Element creation and destruction

When an element is created during an interaction, the communication that creates the element is shown with its arrowhead to the element. When an element is

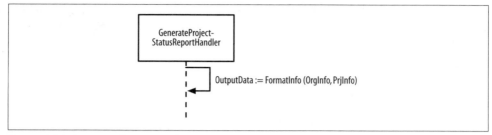

Figure 6-13. Sequence diagram reflexive communications

destroyed during an interaction, the communication that destroys the element is shown with its arrowhead to the element's lifeline where the destruction is marked with a large "X" symbol.

Figure 6-14 shows a communication for step 3 of the Generate Project-Status Report interaction and collaboration description in which the GenerateProject-StatusReportHandler class creates a report. This figure also shows a communication for step 8 of the Generate Project-Status Report interaction and collaboration description where the GenerateProject-StatusReportHandler class destroys the report.

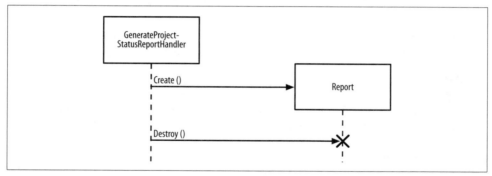

Figure 6-14. Sequence diagram creation and destruction communications

Repetition

In a sequence diagram, repetition (which involves repeating a set of messages or stimuli) within a generic-form interaction is shown as a set of communications enclosed in a rectangle.

An iteration expression may be used at the top-inside or bottom-inside of the rectangle to indicate the number of times the communications inside the rectangle occur. Figure 6-15 shows step 6b of the Generate Project-Status Report interaction and collaboration description using an iteration expression in which the GenerateProject-StatusReportHandler class retrieves the worker's units of work and work products, formats this information, and outputs the formatted information to the report element. Note the use of *[For each worker] in the upper left, which indicates that the communications shown occur once for each worker involved in the project.

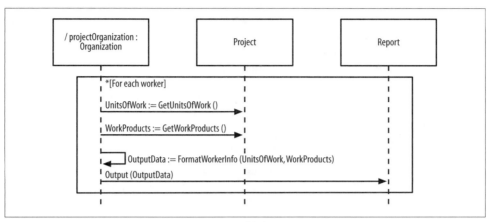

Figure 6-15. Sequence diagram repetition using an iteration expression within a generic-form interaction

Alternatively, a guard expression may be used at the top-inside or bottom-inside of the rectangle to indicate the condition that must be satisfied in order to terminate the repetition. Figure 6-16 shows Figure 6-15 using a guard expression to express the same iteration as in Figure 6-15. Rather than specify explicitly that the set of communications is repeated for each worker, the guard expression specifies that the communications are to be repeated until no more workers remain to be processed.

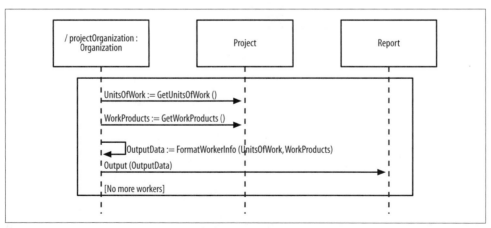

Figure 6-16. Sequence diagram repetition using a guard expression within a generic-form interaction

Repetition within an instance-form interaction involves showing the actual set of messages or stimuli that are repeated. Figure 6-17 shows step 6b of the Generate Project-Status Report interaction and collaboration description (Figure 6-15 and Figure 6-16) for a project that contains exactly three workers, each with two units of work and one work product. Notice that I have also described the interaction in the left margin to make the diagram more readable.

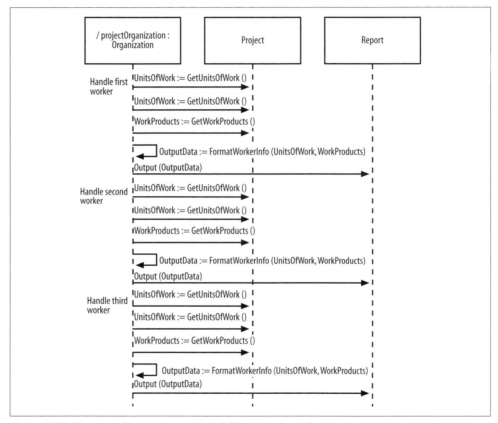

Figure 6-17. Sequence diagram repetition within an instance-form interaction

Conditionality

In a sequence diagram, conditionality (which involves communicating one set of messages or stimuli rather than another set of messages or stimuli) within a generic-form interaction is shown as multiple communications leaving a single point on a lifeline or activation, with the communications having mutually exclusive guard expressions. A lifeline may also split into two or more lifelines to show how a single element would handle multiple incoming communications, and the lifelines would subsequently merge together again.

Figure 6-18 shows steps 5 and 6 of the `Generate Project-Status Report` interaction and collaboration description where the `GenerateProject-StatusReportHandler` class requests that the `projectOrganization` class role indicate that the project is empty if the project is a newly created or unpopulated project, and the `GenerateProject-StatusReportHandler` class requests that the `projectOrganization` class role continue generating information for the report element if the project is not a newly created or populated project. In this figure, only the first communication is shown for actually generating the report. If there are no other communications for actually generating the report, the `GenerateReport` communication may go to the same lifeline as the `OutputEmptyProject` communication. I use different lifelines in the figure because each lifeline represents a different path of execution.

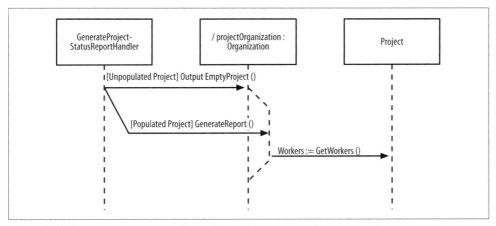

Figure 6-18. Sequence diagram conditionality within a generic-form interaction

Conditionality within an instance-form interaction involves the set of messages or stimuli that are communicated for a specific condition. Figure 6-19 shows Figure 6-18 for a project that is populated.

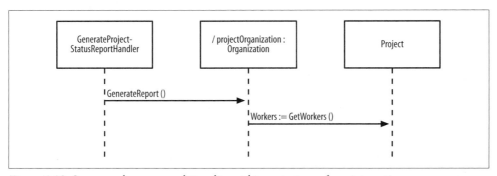

Figure 6-19. Sequence diagram conditionality within an instance-form interaction

Collaboration Diagrams

A collaboration diagram shows elements as they interact over time and how they are related. That is, it shows a collaboration or collaboration instance. While sequence diagrams are time-oriented and emphasize the overall flow of an interaction, collaboration diagrams are time- and space-oriented and emphasize the overall interaction, the elements involved, and their relationships. Sequence diagrams are especially useful for complex interactions, because you read them from top to bottom. Collaboration diagrams are especially useful for visualizing the impact of an interaction on the various elements, because you can place an element on a diagram and immediately see all the other elements with which it interacts.

Elements

Collaboration diagrams are made up of a number of elements, including class roles, specific objects, association roles, and specific links. All of these are described in the following subsections.

Class and association roles

In a collaboration diagram, class roles and other classes are shown using the same notation as in sequence diagrams. An association role is shown using the notation for associations as defined in Chapter 3, but the association name is preceded by a forward slash followed by the name of the role followed by a colon to which links must conform to participate within the role. Other associations may also be shown as necessary using the notation for associations as defined in Chapter 3.

Class roles, association roles, other classes, and other associations are used for specification-level collaborations communicated using collaboration diagrams. Figure 6-20 shows the class roles of Figure 6-8 with the projectReference association role, the Report and Section classes, and the Has association.

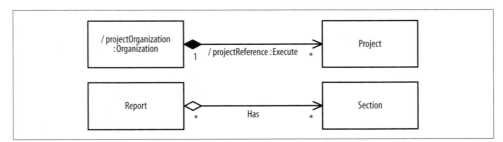

Figure 6-20. Association roles

Specific objects and links

In a collaboration diagram, specific objects conforming to class roles and other objects are shown using the same notation as in sequence diagrams. A specific link of an association conforming to an association role is shown using the notation for links as defined in Chapter 3, but the association name is preceded by a forward slash followed by the name of the role followed by a colon followed by the regular association name, all fully underlined. Recall from Chapter 3 that a link may have its association name shown near the path and is fully underlined, but that links do not have instance names. Other links may also be shown as necessary using the notation for links as defined in Chapter 3.

Specific objects conforming to class roles, specific links conforming to association roles, specific objects, and specific links are used for instance-level collaborations communicated using collaboration diagrams. Figure 6-21 shows the objects of Figure 6-9 with the projectReference link, which is an anonymous Report object with Introduction, Body, and Conclusion objects, and their three Has links.

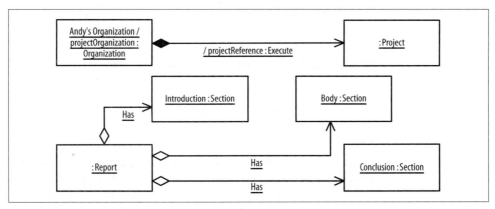

Figure 6-21. Links conforming to association roles

Communication

In a collaboration diagram, a communication, message, or stimulus is shown as an arrow attached to a relationship pointing from the sender toward the receiver. A communication is labeled using the same notation as in sequence diagrams, but a sequence number is required and expressed using a special numbering scheme known as *dot notation* in which a dot or decimal point is used between different levels of communication. For example, between element A and B, communication 1 is followed by communication 2; between element B and C, communication 1.1 is followed by 1.2; and the overall sequence of communication is 1, 1.1, 1.2, and 2.

Figure 6-22 is similar to Figure 6-12, but uses a collaboration diagram to show the communication occurring between the GenerateProject-StatusReportHandler class (which is responsible for managing the overall generation of the report) and the projectOrganization class role.

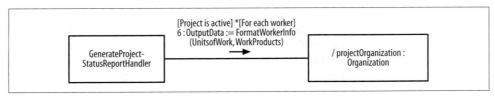

Figure 6-22. Collaboration diagram communications

Reflexive communication

Figure 6-23, similar to Figure 6-13 but using a collaboration diagram, shows a reflexive communication for step 6 of the `Generate Project-Status Report` interaction and collaboration description in which the `GenerateProject-StatusReportHandler` class formats the organization and project information. Notice that a reflexive communication is shown using a reflexive relationship.

Figure 6-23. Collaboration diagram reflexive communications

Element creation and destruction

Figure 6-24, similar to Figure 6-14 but using a collaboration diagram, shows a communication for step 3 of the `Generate Project-Status Report` interaction and collaboration description in which the `GenerateProject-StatusReportHandler` class creates a report. This figure also shows a communication for step 8 of the `Generate Project-Status Report` interaction and collaboration description in which the `GenerateProject-StatusReportHandler` class destroys the report. Notice that a communication that creates an element and a communication that destroys an element are simply shown like any other communication.

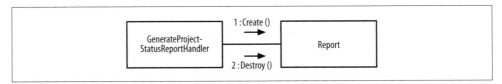

Figure 6-24. Collaboration diagram creation and destruction communications

Repetition

In a collaboration diagram, repetition (which involves repeating a set of messages or stimuli) within a generic-form interaction is shown as a property. Properties are discussed in Chapter 2.

An iteration expression indicating the number of times the communications occur may be enclosed in a pair of braces ({}) and attached to the communications to which it applies using dashed lines. Figure 6-25, similar to Figure 6-15 but using a collaboration diagram, shows step 6b of the Generate Project-Status Report interaction and collaboration description. The figure uses an iteration expression that causes the GenerateProject-StatusReportHandler class to retrieve each worker's units of work and list of work products, to format this information, and to output the formatted information to the report element.

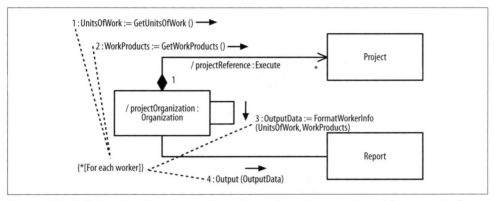

Figure 6-25. Collaboration diagram repetition using an iteration expression within a generic-form interaction

Alternatively, a guard expression indicating the condition that must be satisfied to terminate the repetition may be enclosed in a pair of braces ({}) and attached to the communications to which it applies using dashed lines. Figure 6-26, similar to Figure 6-16 but using a collaboration diagram, uses a guard expression to show the same information as in Figure 6-25.

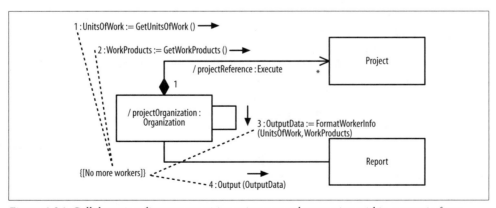

Figure 6-26. Collaboration diagram repetition using a guard expression within a generic-form interaction

Repetition within an instance-form interaction involves showing the actual set of messages or stimuli that are repeated. Figure 6-27, similar to Figure 6-17 but using a collaboration diagram, shows the same information as in Figures 6-25 and 6-26 for a project that contains exactly three workers, each with two units of work and one work product.

Notice that Figure 6-27 may be more difficult to read than Figure 6-17. For more complex interactions, sequence diagrams are often preferable over collaboration diagrams, because sequence diagrams are read from top to bottom. Collaboration diagrams are often preferable over sequence diagrams when the desire is to show the relationships that allow the elements to communicate.

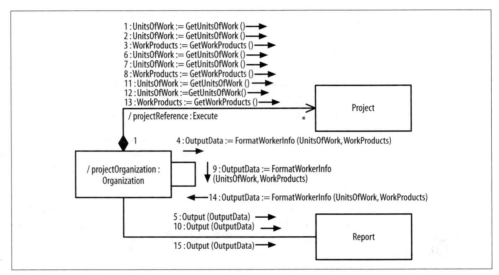

Figure 6-27. Collaboration diagram repetition within an instance-form interaction

Conditionality

In a collaboration diagram, *conditionality*—which involves communicating one set of messages or stimuli rather than another set of messages or stimuli—within a generic-form interaction is shown using the dot notation where the communication at a specific level indicates the guard expression that must be satisfied for the next level of communications to occur. For example, between elements A and B, communication 1 may be labeled with a guard expression and is followed by communication 2. Communication 1 from A to B may trigger communications 1.1 and 1.2 between B and C. Because of the guard condition on communication 1, the following two scenarios are possible:

The guard condition is satisfied

Communication 1 occurs between A and B, triggering 1.1 and 1.2 between B and C. The overall sequence of communications is then 1, 1.1, 1.2, followed by 2. Communication 2 comes last, because everything associated with communication 1 must precede it.

The guard condition is not satisfied

Communication 1 does not occur, and thus neither do communications 1.1 and 1.2. However, communication 2, does occur because it is not protected by the same guard condition as communication 1.

Figure 6-28, similar to Figure 6-18 but using a collaboration diagram, shows steps 5 and 6 of the Generate Project-Status Report interaction and collaboration description where the GenerateProject-StatusReportHandler class requests that the projectOrganization class role indicate that the project is empty if the project is newly created or unpopulated; and the GenerateProject-StatusReportHandler class requests that the projectOrganization class role continue generating information for the report element if the project is not a newly created or populated project. In this figure, only the first communication is shown for actually generating the report.

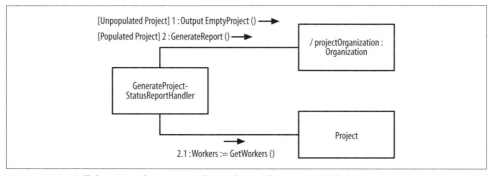

Figure 6-28. Collaboration diagram conditionality within a generic-form interaction

Conditionality within an instance-form interaction involves the set of messages or stimuli that are communicated for a specific condition. Figure 6-29, similar to Figure 6-19 but using a collaboration diagram, shows Figure 6-28 for a project that is populated.

Exercises

1. Figure 6-30 shows a sequence diagram, and Figure 6-31 shows a collaboration diagram. These figures are equivalent; that is, they have the same elements. Identify the missing communications and guard expression and describe the interaction and collaboration. The missing communications in Figure 6-30 are labeled

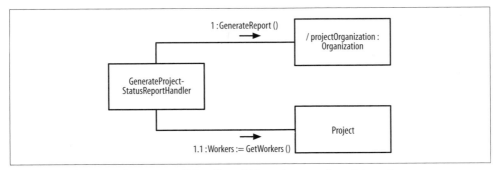

Figure 6-29. Sequence diagram conditionality within an instance-form interaction

ELM-01 and ELM-02. The missing guard expression in Figure 6-30 is labeled ELM-03. The missing communications in Figure 6-31 are labeled ELM-04, ELM-05, and ELM-06.

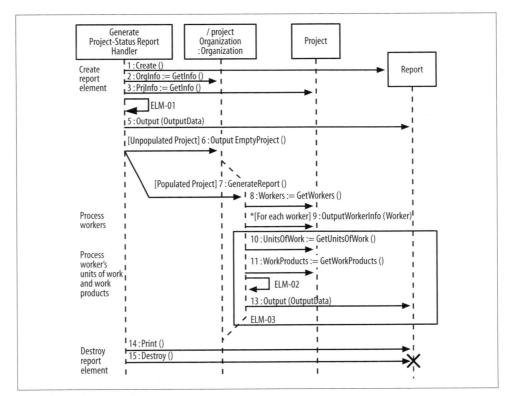

Figure 6-30. Sequence diagram

2. Describe Figures 6-32 and 6-33: identify the various elements. These elements are used for generating a report and its sections.

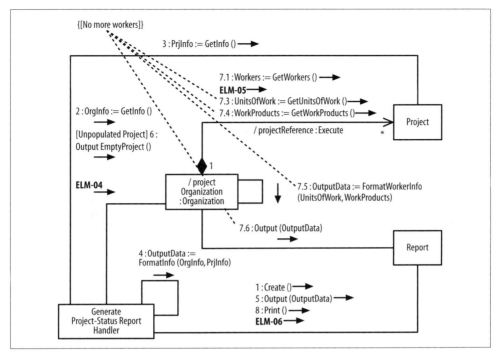

Figure 6-31. *Collaboration diagram*

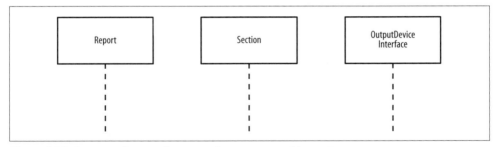

Figure 6-32. *Sequence diagram for generating a report and its sections*

Update the diagrams stepwise to show the following interaction and collaboration. After each step, check your answers against the solutions shown in Appendix B:

a. For each section, the Report element retrieves the section's data using the OutputData := GetData ( ) communication sent to the Section element, and formats the data using the OutputData := FormatData (OutputData) communication sent to itself.

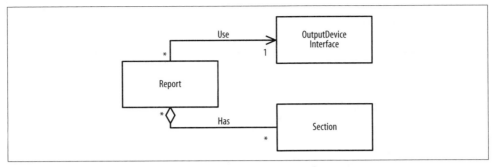

Figure 6-33. Collaboration diagram for generating a report and its sections

b. If the section's data is not summary data, the Report element simply outputs the data to the OutputPrinterInterface element using the OutputNon-SummaryData (OutputData) communication sent to the Output-PrinterInterface element.

c. If the section's data is summary data, the Report element simply outputs the data to the OutputPrinterInterface element using the OutputSummaryData (OutputData) communication sent to the OutputPrinterInterface element.

CHAPTER 7

State Diagrams

This chapter focuses on state diagrams, also known as statechart diagrams, which depict the lifecycle of elements that make up a system. First, I introduce state diagrams and how they are used. Next, I go over states and their details. Finally, I discuss transitions between states and their details. Many details of state diagrams that were not fleshed out in Chapter 2 are more fully elaborated here, and throughout the chapter, I include suggestions relating to state diagrams.

State modeling is a specialized type of behavioral modeling concerned with modeling the lifecycle of an element. You usually apply state modeling in conjunction with interaction and collaboration modeling (Chapter 6) to explore the lifecycle of interacting and collaborating elements.

States

As discussed in Chapter 2, as elements communicate with one another within a society of objects, each element has a *lifecycle* in which it is created, knows something, can do something, can communicate with other elements to request processing of those other elements, can have other elements communicate with it to request processing of it, and is destroyed. A *state* is a specific condition or situation of an element during its lifecycle. Define the states for your elements. The current state of an element is called its *active state*, and the element is said to be "in" that state. There are various types of states, including simple, initial, and final states. The next few sections discuss these different types of states.

Simple States

A *simple state* indicates a condition or situation of an element. For example, the project management system may be in one of the following simple states:

Inactive
> Indicates that the project management system is not available to its users, because it is not started or has been shut down

Active

Indicates that the project management system has been started and is available to its users

Suspended

Indicates that the project management system has encountered some severe error, perhaps because it is running low on secondary storage and requires user intervention before becoming active again

In the UML, a simple state is shown as a rectangle with rounded corners and labeled with the name of the state or a description of the situation of the element. Figure 7-1 shows the various states associated with the project management system.

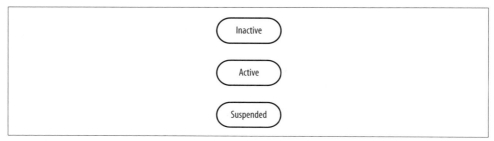

Figure 7-1. Simple states

Initial and Final States

An *initial state* indicates the state of an element when it is created. In the UML, an initial state is shown using a small solid filled circle. A *final state* indicates the state of an element when it is destroyed. In the UML, a final state is shown using a circle surrounding a small solid filled circle (a bull's eye). Figure 7-2 updates Figure 7-1 with an initial state and final state. A state diagram may have only one initial state, but may have any number of final states.

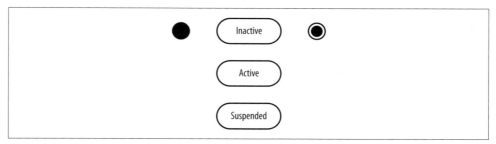

Figure 7-2. Simple, initial, and final states

Transitions

Given the states of an element, how are they related to one another? Transitions address this question. As discussed in Chapter 2, transitions between states occur as follows:

1. An element is in a *source state*.
2. An event occurs.
3. An action is performed.
4. The element enters a *target state*.

When an event occurs, the transition is said to *fire*. In the UML, a transition is shown as a solid line from a source state to a target state labeled with the event followed by a forward slash followed by the action, where the event and action are optional and the forward slash is used only if an action is shown. The next few sections discuss events and actions.

 A transition without an event and action is known as an *automatic transition*. Such transitions are discussed in the next chapter.

Events

An *event* is an occurrence, including the reception of a request. For example, the project management system may respond to the following events:

Startup
> Indicates that the project management system will become active if it is inactive.

Shutdown
> Indicates that the project management system will become inactive if it is active.

Severe Error
> Indicates that the project management system has encountered a severe error, perhaps because it is running low on secondary storage, and will become suspended if it is active.

Reset
> Indicates that the project management system will become active if it is suspended.

In the UML, an event is described using the following UML syntax:

    event_name (parameter_list) [guard]

in which:

event_name
> Is the name of the event. An event usually has the same name as an operation of the element to which the state diagram pertains; therefore when the element receives the event, that operation is invoked.

parameter_list
> Is optional, and is a comma-separated list that indicates the parameters passed to the event. Each parameter may be an explicit value or a variable. The parentheses are not used when the event does not require any parameters.

guard
> Is optional, and indicates a condition that must be satisfied for the transition to fire, or occur. The square brackets are not shown when a guard is not specified.

The UML also allows you to show an event using pseudocode or another language. For example, you can use the syntax of Java, C++, C#, or some other programming language.

Following is an example of an event defined using the syntax just shown. The event informs the project management system to start up:

    Startup

If this event requires the user's identification, you can update the event to the following:

    Startup (*UserID*)

If the project management system responds to this event only if it *can* start up, perhaps if enough memory is available, you can update the transition to the following:

    Startup (*UserID*) [Enough memory is available]

Figure 7-3 shows this transition occurring between the Inactive state, which indicates that the project management system is not available for processing, and the Active state, which indicates that the project management system is available for processing.

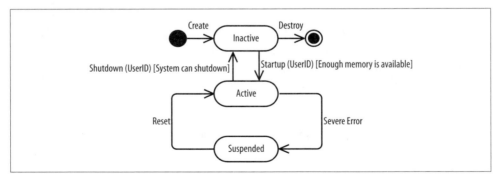

Figure 7-3. Transitions with events

Figure 7-3 also shows a transition originating from the initial state labeled with the event that creates an instance of the project management system and a transition to the final state labeled with the event that destroys an instance of the project management system. Finally, Figure 7-3 shows the various events associated with the project management system, including the Startup, Shutdown, Sever Error, and Reset events.

Actions

An *action* represents processing. For example, the project management system may respond to events with the following actions:

LogMessage

    Indicates that the project management system will log a message in its history file. This file is used for logging the project management system's processing and may be used for diagnosing problems, and so forth.

getDateAndTime

    Indicates that the operating system returns the current date and time from the operating system.

In the UML, an action is described using the following UML syntax:

```
return_variable := target_element.action_name (argument_list)
```

in which:

return_variable

    Is optional, and indicates a name for the value returned by the action to be invoked in response to the event. If you choose not to show a return variable or the action does not return a value, you should omit the succeeding colon and equal sign.

target_element

    Is the name of the element that will perform the action. If the same element that receives the event will perform the action, the target element is not shown and you should omit the succeeding period.

action_name

    Is the name of the action. An action usually has the same name as an operation of the element to which the state diagram pertains, or as an operation of the target element, if one is specified; therefore, when the action is invoked, the element receives the event, and the operation is invoked.

argument_list

    Is optional, and is a comma-separated list that indicates the arguments passed to the action. Each parameter may be an explicit value or a variable. The parentheses are removed when the action does not require any arguments.

The UML also allows you to show an action using pseudocode or another language. For example, you can use the syntax of Java, C++, C#, or some other programming language.

Continuing with the example from the previous section, the following action passes the user's time zone to the operating system (OS) using the getDateAndTime operation:

```
OS.getDateAndTime (TimeZone)
```

If this action returns some output data (the current date and time), you can update the action to the following:

```
DT := OS.getDateAndTime (TimeZone)
```

Figure 7-4 updates Figure 7-3 and shows the events and actions for the transitions between the Inactive and Active states. You can see the logging of a message using the LogMessage action when the system is shut down, and you can see that the Startup event triggers the retrieval of the date and time using the getDateAndTime action of the OS object, which represents the operating system.

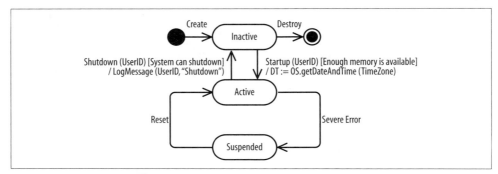

Figure 7-4. Transition with events and actions

Advanced State Diagrams

To be flexible and powerful, the UML allows you to put one or more state diagrams inside a single state to indicate that when an element is in that state, other elements inside of it have their own states. For example, within the Active state of the project management system, each object and subsystem has its own state, and the state diagram for each element may be shown inside the Active state of the project management system or by using the element's own state diagram. This recursive nature of state diagrams is very powerful, because it allows you to learn the basic notation of state diagrams and reapply it to nested state diagrams without having to learn more notation.

In the UML, a state may be shown as a rectangle with rounded corners and three compartments separated by horizontal solid lines. Figure 7-5 shows the Active state of the project management system with three compartments. The top compartment of a state contains the name of the state or a description of the situation of the element.

The middle compartment of a state may contain transitions for the following special events:

entry
    Indicates the action to be performed when the element enters the state

exit
> Indicates the action to be performed when the element exits the state

do
> Indicates the action to be performed continuously while the element is in the state

Figure 7-5 shows that when the project management system enters the Active state, a message is logged using the LogMessage action. When the project management system exits the Active state, the user's date and time is retrieved using the getDateAndTime action of the OS object. Finally, when the project management system is in the Active state, it continuously monitors its usage using the MonitorUsage action.

The bottom compartment of a state may contain one or more nested state diagrams separated by dashed lines, each with a title that describes the element to which the state diagram pertains. When a state becomes the current state of an element, all its nested state diagrams become active concurrently.

Figure 7-5 shows that when the project management system enters the Active state, the following nested state diagrams each has a current state:

Main Graphical User Interface Window or Foreground Processing
> Describes the lifecycle of the user interface. There are two states, including the Shown state, which indicates that the user interface is visible to the user, and the Hidden state, which indicates that the user interface is not visible to the user. The Hide event makes the user interface not visible to the user, and the Show event makes the user interface visible to the user.

Background Processing
> Describes the lifecycle of how the system works as it is handling requests from the user. There are two states, including the Idle state, which indicates that the project management system is not handling any user request, and the Busy state, which indicates that the project management system is handling a user request. The DoProcessing event makes the project management system busy handling a user request, and the ProcessingComplete event makes the project management system idle waiting to handle a user request.

All the transitions going from a state pertain to each nested state diagram; if one of these nested state diagrams activates an outgoing transition, all nested state diagrams are forcibly exited. Figure 7-5 indicates that when the project management system is in the Active state and a Severe Error event occurs, both nested state diagrams are terminated independent of which nested state diagram caused the event to occur.

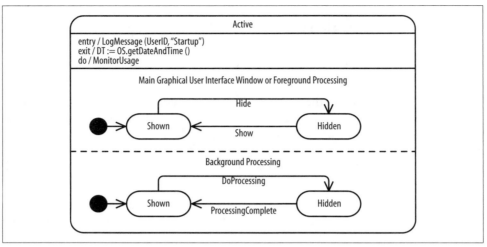

Figure 7-5. Advanced state diagrams

Exercises

1. Describe Figure 7-6, a state diagram that describes the states and transitions between states for a window, as used in Microsoft Windows. Identify the states and transitions shown in the diagram.

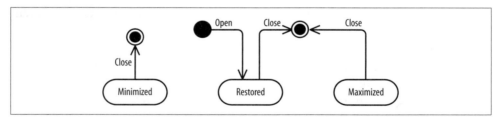

Figure 7-6. States and transitions for a window

2. Update Figure 7-6 stepwise to show the following details. After each step, check your answers against the solutions shown in Appendix B:

   a. If a window receives a Restore event, indicating that the window should be restored or displayed, as one of many windows taking a portion of the space on the user screen, and the window is in the Minimized or Maximized state, it will be changed to the Restored state.

   b. If a window receives a Minimize event, indicating that the window should be minimized or displayed as an icon taking a minimal amount of space on the user screen, and the window is in the Restored or Maximized state, it will be in the Minimized state.

c. If a window receives a `Maximize` event, indicating that the window should be maximized or displayed as the only window taking all the space on the user screen, and the window is in the `Minimized` or `Restored` state, it will be in the `Maximized` state.

d. Every time a window is being restored or maximized it performs a `Redraw` action to render itself.

e. Every time a window is being minimized it requests that the OS reduce its application priority using the `LowPriority` action so that other restored or maximized application windows can have more of the computer's power. The `LowPriority` action requires that the `ApplicationID` argument be passed to it so that the operating system can identify the application whose priority is lower.

CHAPTER 8

Activity Diagrams

This chapter focuses on activity diagrams, which depict the activities and responsibilities of elements that make up a system. First, I introduce activity diagrams and how they are used. Next, I discuss action states and their details. Finally, I go over flows and their details. Many details of activity diagrams that were not fleshed out in Chapter 2 are more fully elaborated here, and throughout the chapter, I include suggestions relating to activity diagrams.

Activity modeling is a specialized type of behavioral modeling concerned with modeling the activities and responsibilities of elements. You usually apply activity modeling in conjunction with sequence and collaboration modeling (Chapter 6) to explore the activities and responsibilities of interacting and collaborating elements.

Action States

As discussed in Chapter 2, as elements communicate with one another within a society of objects, each element has the *responsibility* of appropriately reacting to the communications it receives. An *action state* represents processing as an element fulfills a responsibility. There are various types of action states, including simple, initial, and final action states. The next few sections discuss these different types of action states.

Simple Action States

A *simple action state* represents processing. For example, the project management system may have the following simple action states:

`Project Manager Enters Report Criteria`
  Indicates that the project manager enters report criteria

`Project Management System Generates Report`
  Indicates that the project management system generates a report

`Printer Prints Report`
  Indicates that the printer prints the report

In the UML, an action state is shown as a shape with a straight top and bottom and convex arcs on the two sides, and is labeled with the name of an operation or a description of the processing. Figure 8-1 shows the various action states associated with the project management system.

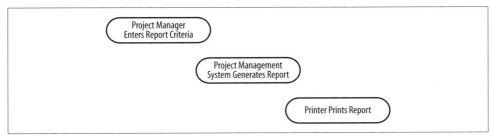

Figure 8-1. Simple action states

Initial and Final Action States

An *initial action state* indicates the first action state on an activity diagram. In the UML, an initial action state is shown using a small solid filled circle. A *final action state* indicates the last action state on an activity diagram. In the UML, a final action state is shown using a circle surrounding a small solid filled circle (a bull's eye). Figure 8-2 updates Figure 8-1 with an initial and final action state. An activity diagram may have only one initial action state, but may have any number of final action states.

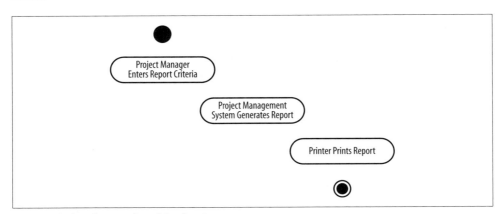

Figure 8-2. Simple, initial, and final action states

Flow Transitions

Given a collection of action states, how are those action states related to one another? Flow transitions address this issue. As discussed in Chapter 2, a *flow transition* shows how action states are ordered or sequenced. There are various types of flow transitions, including control-flow and object-flow transitions, which are mentioned in Chapter 2 and discussed here.

Control-Flow Transitions

A *control-flow transition* indicates the order of action states. That is, once a source action state completes its processing, a target action state starts its processing. For example, the project management system may have the following order of action states for the task of generating a report:

1. The `Project Manager Enters Report Criteria` action state occurs first, because the project manager must enter the report criteria before the system can generate a report.

2. The `Project Management System Generates Report` action state occurs next, because the project management system must generate the report before the printer can print the report.

3. The `Printer Prints Report` action state occurs last, once the report has been generated by the project management system.

In the UML, a control-flow transition is shown as a solid line from a source action state to a target action state. Figure 8-3 shows the order of action states associated with the project management system.

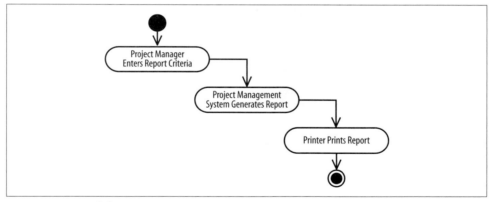

Figure 8-3. Control-flow transitions

Figure 8-3 also shows a control-flow transition originating from the initial state to indicate the first action state, and a transition to the final state to indicate the last action state.

Control-flow transitions are also known as *default transitions* or *automatic transitions*, because they are unlabeled and are immediately triggered after the source action state completes processing.

Object-Flow Transitions

An *object-flow transition* indicates that an action state inputs or outputs an object. For example, the action states shown in Figure 8-3 may have inputs and outputs as follows:

`Project Manager Enters Report Criteria`
  Outputs a `Report Criteria` object and may be renamed as the `Project Manager Enters Data` action state

`Project Management System Generates Report`
  Inputs the `Report Criteria` object and outputs a `Report` object and may be renamed as the `Project Management System Generates Information` action state

`Printer Prints Report`
  Inputs the `Report` object and may be renamed as the `Printer Prints Information` action state

In the UML, an object-flow transition is shown as a dashed arrow between an action state and an object. An action state that uses an object as input is shown with the object-flow transition arrow pointing from the object to the action state. An action state that updates or produces an object as output is shown with the object-flow transition arrow pointing from the action state to the object. Figure 8-4 shows the objects used by the action states associated with the project management system.

Notice the new names for the action states in Figure 8-4 as compared to Figure 8-3. In Figure 8-3, the action state names conveyed some idea of the inputs and outputs from each state. Figure 8-4 however, shows these inputs and outputs explicitly, so there's no longer any need to imply them redundantly in the action state names. The advantage is the action state names can now focus purely on the actions, while the object-flow transitions indicate clearly the inputs and outputs to and from the actions.

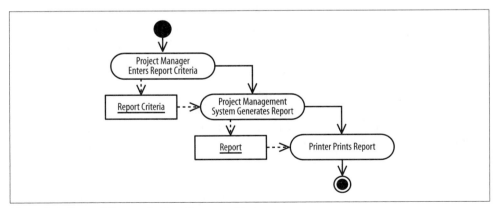

Figure 8-4. Control-flow and object-flow transitions

A control-flow transition may be omitted when an object-flow transition indicates the ordering of action states; that is, when an action state produces an output that is input to a subsequent action state, the object-flow transition implies a control-flow transition and an explicit control-flow transition is not necessary. Figure 8-5 updates Figure 8-4 by removing the unnecessary control-flow transitions.

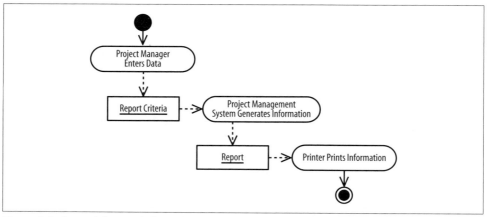

Figure 8-5. Control-flow and object-flow transitions without unnecessary control-flow transitions

Swimlanes

As discussed in Chapter 2, a *swimlane* is a visual region in an activity diagram that indicates the element that has responsibility for action states within the region. For example, the project management system may have the following swimlanes, which are illustrated in Figure 8-6:

Project Manager
> Shows the action states that are the responsibility of a project manager. The swimlane makes it obvious that the project manager is responsible for entering data, thus the rather cumbersome action state name of Project Manager Enters Data may be shortened to Enter Data.

Project Management System
> Shows the action states that are the responsibility of the project management system. Again, because the swimlane makes it obvious who (or what, in this case) is generating information, the rather cumbersome action state name of Project Management System Generates Information may be shortened to Generate Information.

Printer
> Shows the action states that are the responsibility of a printer. Because of this swimlane, the rather cumbersome action state name of Printer Prints Information may be shortened to Print Information.

Notice how the use of swimlanes allows me to rename the action states to omit the responsible element for each action state.

In the UML, a swimlane is shown as a visual region separated from neighboring swimlanes by vertical solid lines on both sides and labeled at the top with the element responsible for action states within the swimlane. Figure 8-6 shows the swimlanes associated with the project management system.

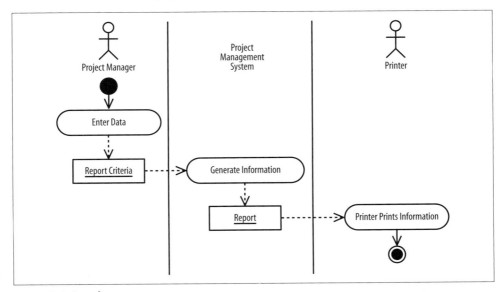

Figure 8-6. Swimlanes

Decisions

A *decision* involves selecting one control-flow transition out of many control-flow transitions based upon a condition. For example, once a report is printed by the project management system, other reports may be selected and printed if the project manager chooses to print more reports.

In the UML, a decision is shown as a diamond shape with incoming control-flow transitions and outgoing control-flow transitions where each outgoing control-flow transition is labeled with a guard condition in square brackets indicating the condition that must be satisfied for the transition to fire, or occur. Figure 8-7 shows that once a report is printed, a project manager may choose to print more reports. Notice that because the diamond shape is in the project manager's swimlane, the project manager is responsible for making the decision.

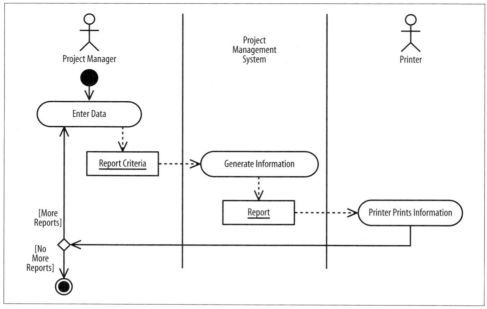

Figure 8-7. Decisions

Concurrency

Concurrency involves selecting multiple transitions simultaneously. For example, while the printer is printing a report, the printer must also monitor for other incoming print requests.

In the UML, concurrency is shown using a short heavy bar. If a bar has one incoming transition and two or more outgoing transitions, it indicates that all outgoing transitions occur once the incoming transition occurs. This is called *splitting of control*. If a bar has two or more incoming transitions and one outgoing transition, it indicates that all incoming transitions must occur before the outgoing transition occurs. This is called *synchronization of control*. Figure 8-8 shows that the printer uses concurrency to print a report using the `Print Information` action state, and to monitor for other incoming print requests while handling the current request using the `Monitor for Print Requests` action state. Once both of these action states have completed, a project manager may choose to print more reports.

Exercises

1. Describe Figure 8-9, an activity diagram that describes the action states and flow transitions between action states for a project manager printing a report using the project management system: identify action states and flow transitions.

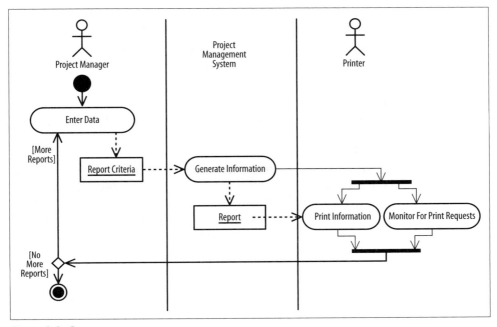

Figure 8-8. Concurrency

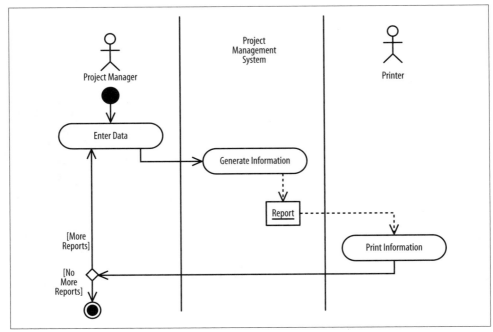

Figure 8-9. Action states and flow transitions for a project manager printing a report

2. Update Figure 8-9 stepwise to show the following details. After each step, check your answers against the solutions shown in Appendix B:

a. The Enter Data action state outputs a Report Criteria object that is then input by the Generate Information action state.

b. The Generate Information action state transitions to the Print Information action state only if the report is successfully generated; otherwise, the project management system generates an error using the Generate Error action state. In either case, the project manager may choose to print more than one report.

c. The project management system must simultaneously generate a report using the Generate Information action state (as well as handle error processing discussed in part b) and execute other processing using the Other Processing action state. Once the report is printed and other processing is handled, the project manager may choose to print more than one report.

PART IV

Beyond the Unified Modeling Language

CHAPTER 9

Extension Mechanisms

This chapter introduces the Unified Modeling Language's extension mechanisms, which allow for extending the language. I discuss how to extend the language using stereotypes, apply the extensions, capture characteristics of model elements using properties, and package extensions using profiles.

As discussed in Chapter 1, a *language* enables us to communicate about a subject, including requirements and the system that satisfies those requirements—for example, the requirements of the project management system that I have been discussing in the book. An extensible language allows us to define new concepts, much like introducing new words and extending the vocabulary of a natural language. For example, rather than have every effort relating to a project management system define the concept of a project, I can extend the UML to incorporate a definition of what a project is, which may be reused by all these other efforts. Also, rather than have every effort relating to a project management system define the relationship between a project and the things that make up a project, I can extend the UML to incorporate a definition of a relationship between a project and the things that make up a project, which may be reused by all these other efforts. Each effort can then specialize these definitions as necessary. For instance, one effort may involve software development projects such as developing an information or technology system, while another effort may involve infrastructure projects such as installing client machines, server machines, and other software. This capability to extend the UML is valuable for creating standardized collections of UML elements that may be reused. Therefore, whenever you find yourself and other people using the same or similar concepts and relationships, as well as reusing these concepts and relationships, you should consider whether you could extend the UML to incorporate these concepts and relationships so that they can be more readily standardized and reused.

Language Architecture

The UML is defined within a scheme called a *four-layer metamodeling architecture* that involves four distinct layers or levels of abstraction. Each layer defines elements, concepts, and relationships between concepts, based on the types of elements in the next more general layer.

For example, consider how we define programming languages and programs using the following layers:

The meta-metamodel or M3-level layer
At the most abstract layer, we define the concepts of data, processing, input, and output where processing inputs and outputs data.

The metamodel or M2-level layer
At the next more specific layer, we can define programming languages that have specific data types and types of processing statements using the concepts of data and processing defined at the M3-level layer. For example, Java has the byte, short, int, long, char, float, and double data types, and it has the if, while, do, for, break, continue, and return processing statements.

The model or M1-level layer
At the next more specific layer, we can define programs that use specific data types and specific processing statements using the types of elements defined at the M2-level layer—for example, a Java program that uses int and char string variables within a for loop to count the number of characters in a string.

The user model or M0-level layer
At the next more-specific layer, we can execute programs—for example, a Java program that counts the number of characters in a string such as "I Love UML," which has 10 characters.

Within this scheme, as each layer has more concrete or specific elements, the "meta" phrase is dropped and the layer number decreases.

For a programming language, the M2-level layer defines the programming language with data types and types of processing statements, the M1-level layer defines a program with specific data variables and specific processing statements using the elements defined in the M2-level layer, and the M0-level layer is an executing program that is defined in the M1-level layer using the data types and types of processing statements defined in the M2-level layer. This is very natural in that an executing program (M0-level layer) is an instance or a specific execution of a defined program (M1-level layer) that uses the data types and types of processing statements of the programming language (M2-level layer).

Similarly, for the UML, we say a model, depicted using class diagrams, is an instance of a metamodel; a user model, depicted using object diagrams, is an instance of a model depicted using class diagrams; a user model, depicted using object diagrams, is an instance of a metamodel; and objects and links are instances of their classes and associations.

This scheme of defining and organizing a language is important in helping us define the language and how it is used; otherwise, a language would be a hodgepodge of different types of modeling elements, concepts, and relationships between concepts, without any thought of how the language is defined and how it may be used.

Similar to how the Java programming language is defined at the metamodel layer, the UML is defined at the metamodel layer as follows:

The meta-metamodel or M3-level layer
> The UML standard defines the notion of a concept.

The metamodel or M2-level layer
> The UML standard defines the concepts of `Class`, `Attribute`, `Operation`, `Object`, `Attribute Value`, `Association`, `Link`, and so forth, which include all the concepts that compose the UML. Each class in the metamodel is known as a *metaclass*.

The model or M1-level layer
> We define specific classes, attributes, operations, and associations—for example, all the classes and associations with all their detail pertaining to the project management system discussed throughout the book.

The user model or M0-level layer
> We define specific objects, attribute values, and links—for example, all the objects and links with all their detail pertaining to the project management system discussed throughout the book.

To ensure that the UML remains standardized, we are unable to modify the metamodel that defines the language. But to ensure that the UML is extensible, we are able to extend the language by defining new concepts using stereotypes, describing them using properties, and packaging and reusing them using profiles.

Stereotypes

A *stereotype* defines a new type of modeling element in the UML. Use stereotypes to define a new type of modeling element and then apply the definition. For example, you might define the concept of a project and the relationship between the project and the things that make up that project.

Defining Stereotypes

In the UML, you create a *stereotype definition* by showing a class representing the stereotype with a dependency on another class representing the type of modeling element the stereotype represents. The class representing the new type of modeling element and the dependency are marked with the `stereotype` keyword, and the class representing the type of modeling element to which the stereotype applies is marked with the `metaclass` keyword. Each class is shown as a solid-outline rectangle marked with the keyword enclosed in guillemets («») or double-angle brackets, before or above its name. The dependency is shown as a dashed arrow from the class representing the stereotype to the other class representing the type of modeling element to which the stereotype applies.

As I discussed in the beginning of this chapter, rather than have many different efforts relating to a project management system define the concept of a project, I can extend the UML to incorporate a definition of what a project is, which may be reused by all these other efforts. Rather than have many different efforts relating to a project management system define the relationship between a project and the things that make up a project, I can extend the UML to incorporate a definition of a relationship between a project and the things that make up a project, which may be reused by all these other efforts. Figure 9-1, a class diagram, defines the concept of a project as a `Project` stereotype, and defines the relationship between a project and the things that make up a project as a `Made Of` stereotype. The `Class` metaclass indicates that the `Project` stereotype applies to classes, and the `Association` metaclass indicates that the `Made Of` stereotype applies to associations.

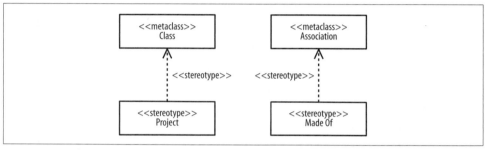

Figure 9-1. Defining stereotypes

Applying Stereotypes

In the UML, you apply a stereotype definition to a model element, then call a *stereotyped element* by showing the name of the new type enclosed in guillemets («») or double-angle brackets, before or above the name of the model element.

Now that I have extended the UML with the concept of a project and the relationship between a project and the things that make it up, I can apply these stereotypes. Figure 9-2, a class diagram, applies the stereotypes defined in Figure 9-1 and shows a development project type named `Development Project`, and an infrastructure project type named `Infrastructure Project`. A development project requires and is made of a development environment, which is described using the `Development Environment` class. An infrastructure project and is made of a deployment environment or platform, which is described using the `Deployment Environment` class. The `Development Project` and `Infrastructure Project` are stereotyped using the `Project` stereotype, and their relationships are stereotyped using the `Made Of` stereotype.

Figure 9-3, an object diagram, applies the stereotypes defined in Figure 9-1, together with the classes and associations defined in Figure 9-2, and shows a development project named `Proj Mngmnt Sys` (which is concerned with developing a project management system), and an infrastructure project named `Java Deployment` (which is

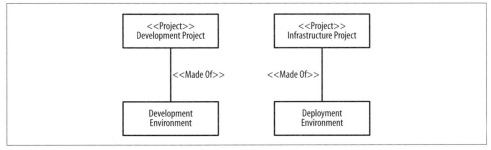

Figure 9-2. Applying stereotypes using class diagrams

concerned with deploying a Java runtime environment). The `Proj Mngmnt Sys` development project is made of the `Java Dev Env` development environment, which provides all the Java tools for developing the project management system. The `Java Deployment` infrastructure project is made of the `UNIX Env` deployment environment, which provides the infrastructure or platform for the Java runtime environment. The objects and links are marked with the same stereotypes as their classes and associations, respectively.

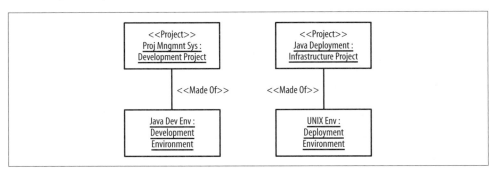

Figure 9-3. Applying stereotypes using object diagrams

Properties

A *property* is a characteristic 1of a model element. Use properties to define attributes and rules for a given type of modeling element. For example, properties can define the following: attributes representing a project's start and end dates, a specific textual description of the relationship between a project and the things that make up the project, and a rule that the start date must precede the end date.

Properties are shown as a comma-delimited list of text strings inside a pair of braces ({}) after or below the name of a model element. Each property may be expressed in any natural or computer language. Each text string may be a tag or constraint, both of which are discussed in the next sections.

Tags

A *tag* is an attribute of a model element and its corresponding value—for example, attributes representing a project's start and end dates.

Defining tags

In the UML, you create a *tag definition* when defining a stereotype by showing a name for the attribute, called a *keyword*, followed by a colon followed by the type of the attribute. The tags defined for a stereotype apply to each model element to which the stereotype is applied.

For example, Figure 9-4 updates Figure 9-1 and shows a tag named Start Date (which is a string representing a project's start date), a tag named End Date (which is a string representing a project's end date), and a tag named Descripton (which is a string representing a description of the relationship between a project and a thing that makes up the project). The Start Date and End Date tags are defined for the Project stereotype, and the Descripton tag is defined for the Made Of stereotype.

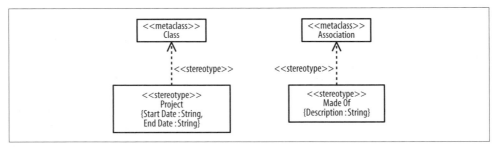

Figure 9-4. Defining stereotypes and tags

Applying tags

In the UML, applying a tag (called a *tagged value*) is done when applying a stereotype by showing the name of the attribute followed by an equal sign followed by its value, together called a *keyword-value pair*. When no equal sign or default value is used, it is assumed that the keyword represents a Boolean value of True, and the absence of the keyword represents a Boolean value of False.

For example, Figure 9-5 updates Figure 9-3 using the tags in Figure 9-4, and shows that the Proj Mngmnt Sys project starts on January 1, 2003 and ends on December 31, 2003. The Java Deployment project starts on December 31, 2003 and ends on January 1, 2003, which is obviously wrong, because the start date is more recent than the end date. Constraints are used to ensure that such errors are not allowed and are discussed in the next section. Figure 9-5 also shows a description for the Proj Mngmnt Sys project's Made Of stereotyped link and indicates that the description for the Java Deployment project's Made Of stereotyped link is empty or blank.

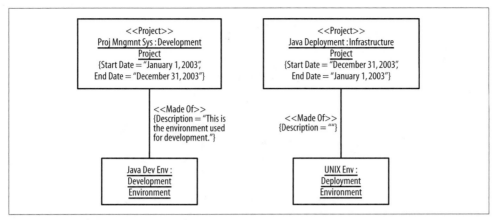

Figure 9-5. Applying stereotypes and tags

Constraints

A *constraint* is a rule for a model element—for example, a rule that a project's start date must precede the project's end date. The rules defined for a stereotype apply to each model element to which the stereotype is applied, and each model element to which the stereotype is applied must adhere to the rules.

In the UML, a constraint is shown when defining a stereotype as a text string that may be expressed using the Object Constraint Language (OCL), which is discussed in Chapter 10. Constraints may also be expressed using pseudocode or another language. For example, you can express a constraint using Java, C++, C#, or some other programming or nonprogramming language.

Figure 9-6 updates Figure 9-4 and shows the following constraint on projects:

```
The End Date must be on or after the Start Date.
```

Figure 9-6 also shows the following constraint on the relationships between a project and the things that make up a project:

```
The Description must not be empty.
```

According to these rules, the `Proj Mngmnt Sys` project described in Figure 9-5 is considered valid. It's start date precedes its end date. On the other hand, the `Java Deployment` project described in Figure 9-5 is considered invalid or erroneous because it starts after it ends.

Profiles

A *profile* is a collection of stereotype definitions, tag definitions, and constraints relevant for a specific domain or purpose. For example, you can group the `Project` and

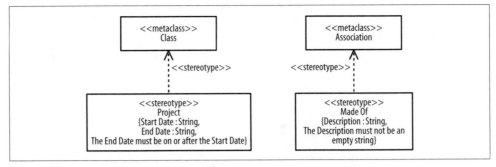

Figure 9-6. Defining stereotypes, tags, and constraints

Made Of stereotypes with their tag definitions and constraints in this chapter into a profile for project management. The project management profile may then be reused when working with other project management systems besides the one in this book.

In the UML, a profile is shown as a package marked with the profile keyword, and a model and all its diagrams may be shown as a package marked with the model keyword. Figure 9-7 shows a Learning UML package, which would contain the diagrams and model elements defined in this book. From that package, you see a dependency to the Project Management profile, which would contain the stereotype definitions, tag definitions, and constraints used for project management, as defined in this chapter. The profiles are packages, as discussed in Chapter 3, and we may show their content on this diagram as well.

The dependency in Figure 9-7 is an *applied profile dependency*. When drawn from a client model package to a supplier profile package, such a dependency indicates that the client model uses the supplier profile; that is, the elements in the model use the elements in the profile. In the UML, an applied profile dependency is shown as a dashed arrow from a client model to a supplier profile marked with the appliedProfile keyword. Figure 9-7 shows that the Learning UML model uses the Project Management profile to define the project management system discussed in this book.

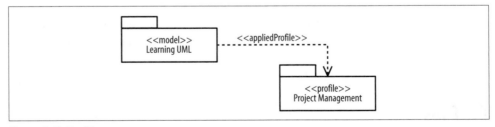

Figure 9-7. Profiles

Exercises

1. Describe Figure 9-8: identify stereotype definitions, tag definitions, and constraints.

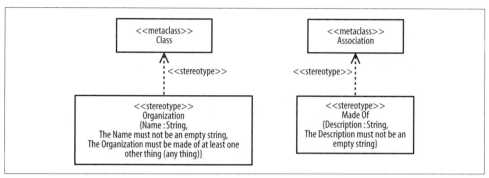

Figure 9-8. Stereotype definitions, tag definitions, and constraints

2. Describe Figure 9-9: identify stereotyped elements and tagged values.

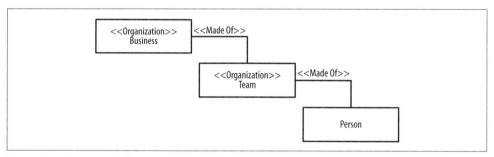

Figure 9-9. Stereotyped elements on a class diagram

3. Describe Figure 9-10: identify stereotyped elements and tagged values.

4. Create a diagram to communicate the following details:

   a. Define the concept of a person using a Person stereotype, which may be applied to classes. The Person stereotype defines a tag named ID, which is a string representing a person's identification number. The ID tag may not be an empty string.

   b. Define the relationship between a person and organization using a Member Of stereotype, which may be applied to associations. The Member Of stereotype defines a tag named Joining Date, which is a string representing the date on which a person joined an organization. The Joining Date may not be an empty string.

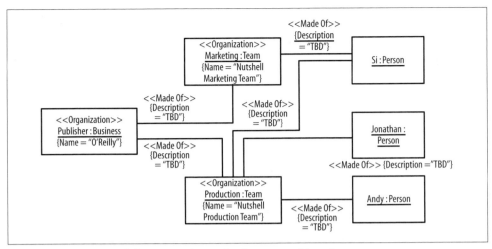

Figure 9-10. Stereotyped elements and tagged values on an object diagram

5. Update the diagram shown in Figure 9-9 stepwise to show the following details. After each step, check your answers against the solutions shown in Appendix B:

   a. A team has members represented using a Member class that is stereotyped as a Person rather than a Team class.

   b. Objects of the Member class are associated with teams represented using an association that is stereotyped using the Member Of stereotype rather than the Made Of stereotype.

6. Update the diagram shown in Figure 9-10 stepwise to show the following details. After each step, check your answers against the solutions shown in Appendix B:

   a. All Person class objects become Member class objects stereotyped using the Person stereotype. The Andy object's ID tag has a tagged value of 1. The Jonathan object's ID tag has a tagged value of 2. The Si object's ID tag has a tagged value of 3.

   b. All Person class objects become members of teams using associations stereotyped using the Member Of stereotype, and each of the links has a tagged value of TBD (to be determined) for the Description tag.

CHAPTER 10

The Object Constraint Language

This chapter introduces the UML's Object Constraint Language (OCL), a sublanguage of the UML that allows for capturing constraints or rules and attaching them to model elements, which then must satisfy the constraints for the model to be considered correct (also known as *well formed*). I discuss how to express rules as expressions and how to attach those rules to model elements as properties. As the OCL is a complete language in its own right, this chapter does not discuss every aspect of the OCL, as that would require a whole different book. Instead, this chapter focuses on simply introducing you to the OCL. For further information beyond this chapter, please see Appendix A for references to notable resources on the World Wide Web and various books that further discuss the OCL.

For example of how the OCL might be used, recall that in Chapter 9 I discussed how a model is erroneous if a project's start date succeeds its end date. I pointed out that a project's start date must precede its end date. In Chapter 9, I captured this and other rules using natural human language, but we can use the OCL to more formally capture such rules. Capturing such rules more formally is valuable, because we can begin to automate the checking of the correctness of UML models.

Expressions

As discussed in Chapter 9, a *property* is a characteristic of a model element shown as part of a comma-delimited list of text strings inside a pair of braces ({}) after or below the name of a model element, and a *constraint* is a rule for a model element shown as a text string within the property list. An OCL *expression* is a constraint that yields a value when evaluated. An *invariant* is an expression attached to a model element that must hold true for all instances of that model element. That is, an expression attached to a class means that each object of the class must satisfy the expression, and an expression attached to an association means that each link of the association must satisfy the expression. When an expression is evaluated for a specific object or link, the object or link is known as the *contextual instance*, and the optional keyword self in an expression refers to that contextual instance.

An OCL expression is evaluated from left to right. For an expression attached to an object, the expression may reference its attributes and tags, side effect–free operations, links and link objects, and the objects with which it is linked through the link ends of its links. For an expression attached to a link, the expression may reference its attributes and tags, side effect–free operations, and the objects it links through its link ends. A *side effect–free operation* is an operation that does not modify the attributes of an object or link, but may calculate and return a value. As each part of an expression is evaluated, each intermediate resulting value may be a single object or a collection of objects called a *collection* that is further used in the evaluation of the overall expression.

Expressions may involve integers and real numbers, strings, and other objects defined in a model. For integers and real numbers, you can use the arithmetic operators and comparison operators shown in Table 10-1. For strings, you can use the = operator for "equal to" and the <> operator for "not equal to." In addition, expressions may use the logical operators, also shown in Table 10-1. As an expression is evaluated from left to right, the unary operators have the highest precedence, followed by the arithmetic operators, and then followed by the logical operators. These operations are used in the OCL much the way they are used in Java, C++, C#, or any other similar programming language with which you may be familiar.

 For strings, the UML supports the = operator for "equal to" and the <> operator for "not equal to." The UML does not support the < or > operator for strings.

Table 10-1. Operators of the OCL

Type	Operator	Description
Arithmetic	+	Addition
	-	Subtraction and unary minus
	*	Multiplication
	/	Division
Comparison	<	Less than
	>	Greater than
	<=	Less than or equal to
	>=	Greater than or equal to
	<>	Not equal to
	=	Equal to
Logical operators	Not	Unary not
	And	And
	Or	Or
	Xor	Exclusive or

Figure 10-1 shows various relationships among organizations, projects, teams, people, and people's roles on teams in the project management system. An organization relates to zero or more projects, zero or more teams, and zero or more people who are employees of the organization. A project relates to a single organization and to a single team. A team relates to a single organization and to a single project. A person relates to a single organization that is an employer. A team relates to zero or more people as members of the team in which a person plays a role. A person relates to a single team in which the person plays a role.

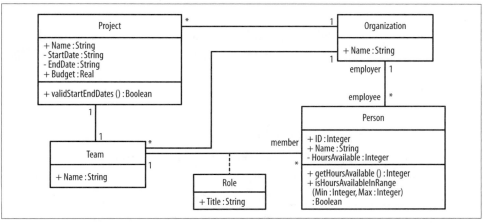

Figure 10-1. Organizations, projects, teams, and people

Figure 10-1 also shows various details about organizations, projects, teams, people, and people's roles on teams in the project management system. A project has a name that is a string, a start date that is a string, an end date that is a string, a budget that is a real number, and an operation to ensure that the start date and end date of the project are valid (that the project's start date precedes its end date). Each team and organization has a name that is a string. A person has an identification number that is an integer, a name that is a string, hours that they are available to work presented as an integer, an operation to retrieve the number of hours that they are available to work, and an operation to determine whether the number of hours that they are available to work is within a range of a minimum and maximum number of hours. The relationship between a person and a team defines the title as a string of the role that the person plays on the team. All the attributes and operations are public, but a project's start and end date and the hours they are available to work are private.

I'll use Figure 10-1 throughout the remainder of this chapter as the basis for showing you how to apply the OCL.

Simple Constraints

Simple constraints that involve one object, or two objects and their link, provide the foundation for working with more complex constraints that involve multiple objects and their links.

Attributes

To specify a rule about the values of an object's attributes, you can refer to an object's attribute from the object itself by using the name of the attribute.

Within the context of an organization, the following expression indicates that the name of an organization may not be an empty string:

```
Name <> ''
```

Using the keyword `self`, this rule may be described as follows:

```
self.Name <> ''
```

Notice that a literal string is enclosed in single quotes.

Figure 10-2 updates Figure 10-1 to show how the rule is captured. Look specifically at the top compartment for `Organization`.

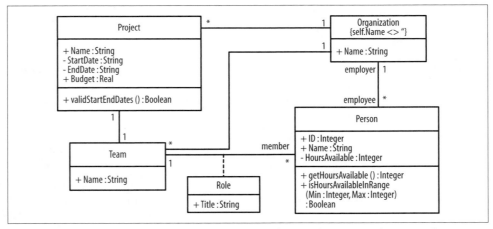

Figure 10-2. Organizations with an OCL expression indicating that organizations must have names

Within the context of a person, the following expression indicates that a person must work more than 10 hours and less than or equal to 40 hours:

```
HoursAvailable > 10 and HoursAvailable <= 40
```

Using the keyword `self`, this rule may be described as follows:

```
self.HoursAvailable > 10 and self.HoursAvailable <= 40
```

Notice that the keyword self is used at the beginning of each occurrence of the HoursAvailable attribute. Also notice that I can access this attribute even though it is private, because the expression is written within the context of a person. If the context of the rule is not a person object, I would not be able to access the attributes directly in the expression.

Operations

To specify a rule that uses an object's operations, you can refer to an object's operation from the object itself by using the name of the operation followed by parentheses containing an optional comma-separated list that specifies the actual parameters passed to the operation. If the operation does not have any parameters, the parentheses are mandatory and left empty.

Within the context of a project, the following expression uses the valid-StartEndDates operation to check that the start and end dates are valid:

```
validStartEndDates ( )
```

Using the keyword self, this rule may be described as follows:

```
self.validStartEndDates ( )
```

Notice that because the operation returns a Boolean value, I did not have to compare it to anything. If the operation returns a value of True, the rule is satisfied. If the operation returns a value of False, the rule is not satisfied.

Link Ends

As discussed in Chapter 3, a *link end* is an endpoint of a link that connects the link to an object.

To refer to an object across a link, use the rolename attached to the link end. If the link end does not have a rolename, use the class name of the object of the link end, but start the class name with a lowercase character.

Link ends with a multiplicity of 1

Within the context of a person, the following partial expression returns the organization related to the person using the rolename attached to the link end:

```
self.employer
```

Within the context of a project, the following partial expression returns the organization related to the project using the class name of the object of the link end, but starting with a lowercase character:

```
self.organization
```

In these two expressions referring to a person's organization and a team's organization, because the multiplicity on the association end related to the link end attached to the Organization class has a maximum of 1, the result is an object of the class connected to the link end. That is, each previous expression results in a single object of the Organization class. Also notice that I used the class name to refer to the organization from the project, but I used the rolename to refer to the organization from the person. You can use the class name if no rolename is specified; otherwise, you can use the rolename.

To refer to a characteristic of a single object, use a dot. Within the context of a person, the following expression indicates that the name of the organization related to a person cannot be an empty string:

```
self.employer.Name <> ''
```

Within the context of a project, the following expression indicates that the name of the organization related to a project cannot be an empty string:

```
self.organization.Name <> ''
```

Link ends with a multiplicity of more than 1

Within the context of an organization, the following partial expression returns the collection of people related to an organization using the rolename attached to the link end:

```
self.employee
```

Within the context of an organization, the following partial expression returns the collection of projects related to an organization using the class name (starting with a lowercase character) of the objects at the link end:

```
self.project
```

In these two expressions referring to an organization's people and an organization's projects, because the multiplicity on the association ends related to the link ends attached to the People class and Project class have no maximum or have a maximum of more than 1, the result is a set collection of objects of the class connected to the link end. Such a set is a collection of unique and unordered objects. That is, the first expression above results in a set of objects of the Person class and the second expression results in a set of objects of the Project class.

To refer to a characteristic of a collection, use an arrow (->). Within the context of an organization, the following expression indicates that the names of the people related to an organization may not be an empty string:

```
self.employee->forAll (e : Person | e.Name <> '')
```

The forAll in this expression indicates a rule that must be satisfied by each element of the set of employees. The first part of the expression enclosed in the parentheses indicates that each element of the set is a person that is referenced using the variable e. The second part of the expression, which is separated from the first part by a vertical bar (|), indicates the rule that each element of the set must satisfy. If any employee has an empty name, the result of the forAll is False; otherwise, the result is True.

Within the context of an organization, the following expression indicates that the names of the projects related to an organization cannot be an empty string:

```
self.project->forAll (p : Project | p.Name <> '')
```

The forAll in this expression indicates a rule that must be satisfied by each element of the set of projects. The first part of the expression enclosed in the parentheses indicates that each element of the set is a project that is referenced using the variable p. The second part of the expression, which is separated from the first part by a vertical bar (|), indicates the rule that each element of the set must satisfy. If any project has an empty name, the result of the forAll is False; otherwise, the result is True.

Within the context of an organization, the following expression indicates that each person who is employed by an organization must work more than 10 hours and less than or equal to 40 hours:

```
self.employee->forAll (e : Person | e.isHoursAvailableInRange (10, 40))
```

Notice that I must use the isHoursAvailableInRange operation, and that I cannot use the HoursAvailable attribute because it is private to the person objects and not accessible from the context of an organization.

Link Objects

As discussed in Chapter 3, a *link object* is a specific instance of an association that links multiple objects.

Given a link and the objects it relates, you can refer to a link object from the objects that are linked, and you can refer to the objects that are linked from the link object.

Referring to link objects

To refer to link objects from an object on one end of a link, use the class name of the link object, but starting with a lowercase character, which results in a set collection of objects of the link's class.

Within the context of a team or a person, the following expression indicates that the title of each role object of a team or a person may not be an empty string:

```
self.role->forAll (r : Role | r.Title <> '')
```

Notice that this expression may be used within the context of a team or a person, because it references the links between teams and people.

Referring to linked object

To refer to the object of a link end from a link object, use the rolename attached to the link end. If the link end does not have a rolename, use the class name of the object of the link end, but starting with a lowercase character, which results in exactly one object.

Within the context of a role, the following expression indicates that the name of the team to which a role applies may not be an empty string using the class name:

```
self.team.Name <> ''
```

Within the context of a role, the following expression indicates that the name of the person to which a role applies may not be an empty string using the rolename:

```
self.member.Name <> ''
```

Notice that these are two different expressions used within the context of a role, because each expression references a different link end.

Complex Constraints

Complex constraints involve multiple objects and their links, and capture more complex rules than are shown in the previous section on simple constraints. Multiplicity constraints are a special case of complex constraints in that they have their own notation; you do not need to capture multiplicity constraints using the OCL.

Multiplicity notation is used in Figure 10-1's class diagram to define multiplicity rules that must be respected. One such constraint states that a project relates to a single organization and to a single team. Figure 10-3 shows an object diagram that is invalid because it violates those rules.

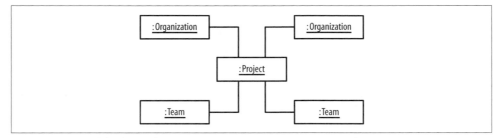

Figure 10-3. Invalid relationships between organizations, a project, and teams

The UML's multiplicity notation captures rules regarding the number of objects that may be related to one another. However, using the OCL, many other complex rules may be expressed using constraints.

 You could capture multiplicity constraints using the OCL, but instead you should use the notation for such constraints already built into the UML.

Figure 10-1 shows the details about organizations, projects, teams, and people, but does not indicate whether a project and its team must relate to the same organization, nor does it indicate whether a team and its members must relate to the same

---

organization. Using the OCL, it's possible to create a complex constraint that enforces the rule that a project, its team, and all the team members must belong to one organization.

Figure 10-4 shows a project and a team that relate to one another and to two different organizations. This would allow a team to work on a project for another organization, which most organizations don't allow! Let's look at how we can use the OCL to prevent the situation in Figure 10-4 from occurring.

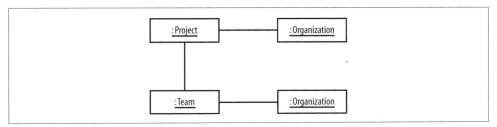

Figure 10-4. Relationships between organizations, a project, and a team

There are multiple expressions to show that a project and a team that relate to one another must relate to the same organization.

Within the context of a team, I can use the following expression to assert that the project's organization must match the team's organization:

```
self.project.organization = self.organization
```

Coming at it from the other direction, within the context of a project, I can use the following expression to express the same rule:

```
self.team.organization = self.organization
```

Within these expressions, the keyword self is optional and the expressions on either side of the = symbol may be interchanged. For example, the following two expressions produce identical results:

```
self.team.organization = self.organization
self.organization = self.team.organization
```

Keep in mind that if you use less than (<) or greater than (>) in an expression, you cannot interchange the expressions on either side of the operator.

Figure 10-5 shows how the rule is captured in Figure 10-1.

Now consider how these rules can be expressed in the context of an organization. The following rule ensures that every team related to an organization's project is related to the same organization:

```
organization.project->forAll (p : Project | p.team.organization = self)
```

The following rule ensures that every project related to an organization's team is related to the same organization:

```
organization.team->forAll (t : Team | t.project.organization = self)
```

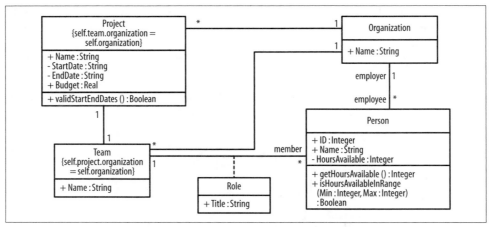

Figure 10-5. Organizations, projects, teams, and people with another OCL expression

Notice that the self keyword is not optional in these two expressions because it is the only way for an organization object to refer to itself.

Figure 10-6 illustrates another potential problem, showing a team and a person that relate to one another but that also relate to two different organizations. This allows a person to work on a team for another organization, which most employers don't allow! Thus, we reasonably might want to write a constraint prohibiting the situation.

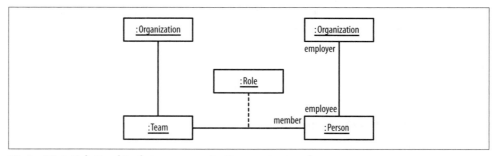

Figure 10-6. Relationships between organizations, a team, and a person

Consider how a team and a person relate to one another. For example, a team and a person that relate to one another ought to relate to the same organization. Within the context of a team, I can use one of the following expressions to capture this rule between teams, people, and their organization:

```
self.member->forAll (m : Person | m.organization = self.organization)
self.person->forAll (p : Person | p.organziation = self.organization)
```

Notice that because there are many members of a team, I used the `forAll` in this expression to indicate that the rule must be satisfied by each element of the set of team members.

Within the context of a person, I can use one of the following expressions to capture this rule between teams, people, and their organization:

```
self.team.organization = self.organization
self.team.organziation = self.employeer
```

Again, within these expressions, the keyword `self` is optional and the expressions on either side of the = symbol may be interchanged. You cannot interchange expressions on either side of the < or > symbols.

The multiplicities discussed in the previous section and the rules discussed in this section make the model more precise in representing how organizations, projects, teams, and people are related to one another.

Exercises

1. Describe Figure 10-7: identify classes and associations, including their attributes and operations.

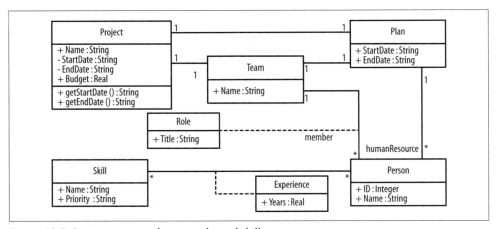

Figure 10-7. Projects, teams, plans, people, and skills

2. With respect to Figure 10-7, describe the following rules:

    a. Within the context of a skill:

    ```
    self.Priority = "High" or self.Priority = "Medium" or self.Priority = "Low"
    ```

    b. Within the context of a project:

    ```
    self.Budget >= 100000 and Budget <= 500000
    ```

    c. Within the context of a role:

    ```
    self.team.Name <> ''
    ```

d. Within the context of a role:

```
self.member.ID > 0 and self.person.ID < 9999
```

e. Within the context of a team:

```
self.member->forAll (p : Person | p.ID > 0 and p.ID < 9999)
```

f. Within the context of a team:

```
self.person->forAll (p : Person | p.ID > 0 and p.ID < 9999)
```

g. Within the context of a team:

```
self.plan.humanResource->forAll (p : Person | p.ID > 0 and p.ID < 9999)
```

3. Describe how to capture the following rules using Figure 10-7.

   a. Within the context of a role, a title must be one of the following: Analyst, Architect, Designer, Developer, Tester, or Manager.

   b. Within the context of experience, a person must have at least five years of experience.

   c. Within the context of a project, its start and end dates must match its plan's start and end dates.

   d. Within the context of a plan, its start and end dates must match its project's start and end dates.

   e. Within the context of a person, a person and a team that relate to one another must relate to the same plan.

   f. Within the context of a person, a person, team, and project that relate to one another must relate to the same plan.

   g. Within the context of a team, the plan that relates to the team and the project that relates to the team must be related to one another.

Appendixes

References

This appendix contains references to notable UML resources on the World Wide Web and to various books.

World Wide Web

The following web sites are the primary sources for the UML standard:

http://www.omg.org and http://www.omg.org/uml
    The Object Management Group (OMG)

http://www.rational.com and http://www.rational.com/uml
    Rational Software Corporation

The following web sites offer other worthwhile information regarding the OCL, the next major revision of the UML, and a virtual community:

http://www.klasse.nl/ocl/index.htm
    The Object Constraint Language (OCL).

http://www.u2-partners.org
    The U2 Partners are focusing on the next major revision of the UML.

http://www.uml-forum.com
    The UML Forum is a virtual community concerning the UML.

The following web sites offer other worthwhile information regarding improving the UML:

http://www.2uworks.org
    The 2U Consortium.

http://www.cs.york.ac.uk/puml
    The Precise UML (pUML) Group.

The following web sites offer other worthwhile information and links:

http://home.earthlink.net/~salhir
    Sinan Si Alhir's personal web site.

http://www.cetus-links.org
    The Cetus Team offers significant information regarding UML tools, methodologies, processes, and much more.

Books

The following document is the primary source for the UML standard:

- The Object Management Group (OMG). *OMG Unified Modeling Language Specification (Action Semantics)* (Version 1.4). The Object Management Group (OMG), 2001.

The following books offer a reference to the UML and a practical tool-, process-, and technology-independent road map for effectively and successfully applying the UML:

- Sinan Si Alhir. *UML in a Nutshell: A Desktop Quick Reference*. O'Reilly & Associates, 1998.
- Sinan Si Alhir. *Guide to Applying the UML*. Springer-Verlag, 2002.

The following articles offer a good reference to the UML and Unified Process:

- Sinan Si Alhir. The Unified Modeling Language (UML). In John J. Marciniak (ed.): *Encyclopedia of Software Engineering*, Second Edition. John Wiley & Sons, 2001.
- Sinan Si Alhir. The Unified Process (UP). In John J. Marciniak (ed.): *Encyclopedia of Software Engineering*, Second Edition. John Wiley & Sons, 2001.

The following books by the *Three Amigos* offer a simple tutorial to the UML, a reference that mimics the OMG document, and their thoughts on process:

- Grady Booch, James Rumbaugh, and Ivar Jacobson. *The Unified Modeling Language User Guide*. Addison Wesley, 1999.
- James Rumbaugh, Ivar Jacobson, and Grady Booch. *The Unified Modeling Language Reference Manual*. Addison Wesley Longman, 1999.
- Ivar Jacobson, Grady Booch, and James Rumbaugh. *The Unified Software Development Process*. Addison Wesley Longman, 1999.

The following book by Jos Warmer and Anneke Kleppe offers more detail on the OCL:

- Jos Warmer and Anneke Kleppe. *The Object Constraint Language: Precise Modeling with UML*. Addison Wesley Longman, 1999.

Exercise Solutions

This appendix contains solutions to the exercises. Note that for many problems, there may be multiple viable solutions.

For exercise questions involving figures, the figures for each step show only the solution for that particular step and not for the whole question (which would include the solutions to previous steps in the question). At the end of each question, all the figures for all the steps in the question are combined to produce a final solution to the question.

Structural Modeling

The next few sections present solutions for Part II.

Chapter 3, *Class and Object Diagrams*

1. The figure shows a Report class.

    The class has the following attributes:

    - NextID, which is private, holds an integer value, is initialized to 1, and is shared by all the objects of the class.

    - ID, which is private, holds an integer value, is not initialized to any value, and is specific to each object of the class.

    - Name, which is private, holds a string value, is initialized to an empty string, and is specific to each object of the class.

    - CreationDate, which is private, holds a string value, is initialized to an empty string, and is specific to each object of the class.

    - SectionName, which is private, holds one or more ordered string values that are initialized to an empty string, and is specific to each object of the class.

- ProjectName, which is private, holds one or more unordered string values that are initialized to an empty string, and is specific to each object of the class.

- OwnerName, which is private, holds a string value, is not initialized to any value, and is specific to each object of the class.

The class has the following operations:

- create, which is public, receives no parameters, returns a value of type Report, and applies to the class rather than a specific object of the class.

- create, which is public, receives one parameter, returns a value of type Report, and applies to the class rather than a specific object of the class. The operation receives a parameter named theOwnerName, which is input and may not be modified by the operation, holds a string value, and is initialized to the string "Unknown Owner".

- destroy, which is public, receives no parameters, returns nothing, and applies to objects of the class.

- getID, which is public, receives no parameters, returns an integer value, and applies to objects of the class.

- setName, which is public, receives one parameter, returns nothing, and applies to objects of the class. The operation receives a parameter named theName, which is input and may not be modified by the operation, holds a string value, and is not initialized to any value.

- getName, which is public, receives no parameters, returns a string value, and applies to objects of the class.

- getCreationDate, which is public, receives no parameters, returns a string value, and applies to objects of the class.

- setSectionName, which is public, receives two parameters, returns nothing, and applies to objects of the class. The first parameter that the operation receives is named theSectionName, which is input and may not be modified by the operation, holds a string value, and is not initialized to any value. The second parameter that the operation receives is named theSectionOrder, which is input and may not be modified by the operation, holds an integer value, and is initialized to the value 1.

- getSectionName, which is public, receives one parameter, returns a string value, and applies to objects of the class. The operation receives a parameter named theSectionOrder, which is input and may not be modified by the operation, holds an integer value, and is initialized to the value 1.

- addProjectName, which is public, receives one parameter, returns nothing, and applies to objects of the class. The operation receives a parameter named theProjectName, which is input and may not be modified by the operation, holds a string value, and is not initialized to any value.

- `removeProjectName`, which is public, receives one parameter, returns nothing, and applies to objects of the class. The operation receives a parameter named `theProjectName`, which is input and may not be modified by the operation, holds a string value, and is not initialized to any value.

- `setOwnerName`, which is protected, receives one parameter, returns nothing, and applies to objects of the class. The operation receives a parameter named `theOwnerName`, which is input and may not be modified by the operation, holds a string value, and is not initialized to any value.

- `getOwnerName`, which is protected, receives no parameters, returns a string value, and applies to objects of the class.

- `doesReportHaveProjectName`, which is public, receives one parameter, returns a Boolean value, and applies to objects of the class. The operation receives a parameter named `theProjectName`, which is input and may not be modified by the operation, holds a string value, and is not initialized to any value.

- `setNameAndOwner`, which is public, receives two parameters, returns nothing, and applies to objects of the class. The first parameter that the operation receives is named `theName`, which is input and may not be modified by the operation, holds a string value, and is not initialized to any value. The second parameter that the operation receives is named `theOwnerName`, which is input and may not be modified by the operation, holds a string value, and is not initialized to any value. An operation named `getNameAndOwner`, which is public, receives two parameters, returns nothing, and applies to objects of the class. The first parameter that the operation receives is named `theName`, which is output and may be modified by the operation, holds a string value, and is not initialized to any value. The second parameter that the operation receives is named `theOwnerName`, which is output and may be modified by the operation, holds a string value, and is not initialized to any value.

- `refreshNameAndOwner`, which is public, receives two parameters, returns nothing, and applies to objects of the class. The first parameter that the operation receives is named `theName`, which is input and may be modified by the operation, holds a string value, and is not initialized to any value. The second parameter that the operation receives is named `theOwnerName`, which is input and may be modified by the operation, holds a string value, and is not initialized to any value.

2. The figure shows a `Report` object named `ProjectAndTeamStatus`, described in the following:

   - The object's `ID` attribute has the integer value of 1.
   - The object's `Name` attribute has the string value of "Project Report".
   - The object's `CreationDate` attribute has the string value of "January 2002".

- The object's `SectionName` attribute has the ordered string values of "Project Information", "Status Information", and "Team Information".
- The object's `ProjectName` attribute has the unordered string values of "Eagle", "Falcon", and "Hawk".
- The object's `OwnerName` attribute has the string value "Nora".

3. The following describes the figure: workers and skills are related, projects and activities are related, and activities and skills are related.

   a. Figure B-1 shows the figure.

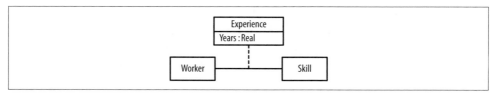

Figure B-1. Class diagram (question 3 part a)

   b. Figure B-2 shows the figure.

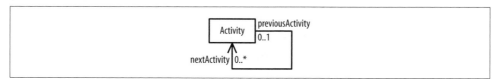

Figure B-2. Class diagram (question 3 part b)

   c. Figure B-3 shows the figure.

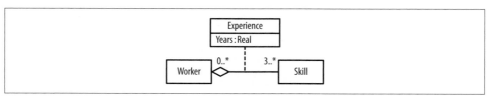

Figure B-3. Class diagram (question 3 part c)

   d. Figure B-4 shows the figure.

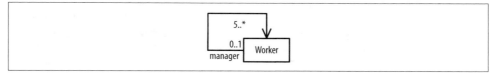

Figure B-4. Class diagram (question 3 part d)

e. Figure B-5 shows the figure.

Figure B-5. Class diagram (question 3 part e)

f. Figure B-6 shows the figure.

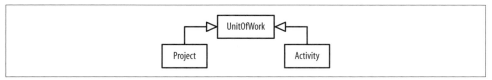

Figure B-6. Class diagram (question 3 part f)

Figure B-7 shows the resulting diagram, which includes all the steps in this question.

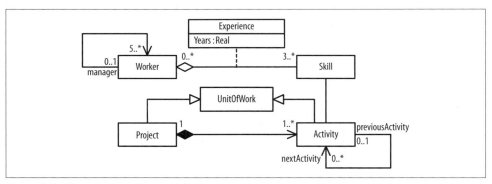

Figure B-7. Class diagram (question 3)

4. The following describes the figure: a plan relates workers and activities on a project.

a. Figure B-8 shows the figure.

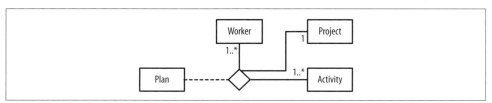

Figure B-8. Class diagram (question 4 part a)

b. Figure B-9 shows the figure.

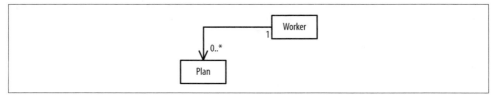

Figure B-9. Class diagram (question 4 part b)

c. Figure B-10 shows the figure.

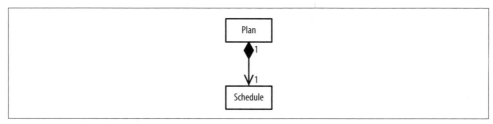

Figure B-10. Class diagram (question 4 part c)

d. Figure B-11 shows the figure.

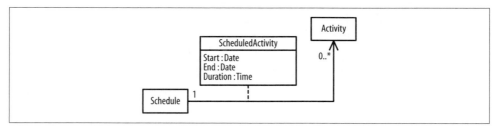

Figure B-11. Class diagram (question 4 part d)

e. Figure B-12 shows the figure.

Figure B-13 shows the resulting diagram, which includes all the steps in this question.

5. The following figures result:

a. Figure B-14 results from the description.

b. Figure B-15 results from the description.

c. Figure B-16 results from the description.

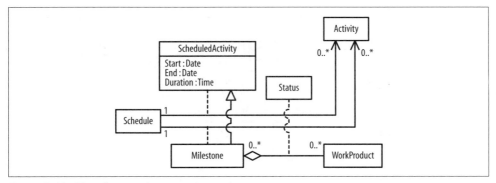

Figure B-12. Class diagram (question 4 part e)

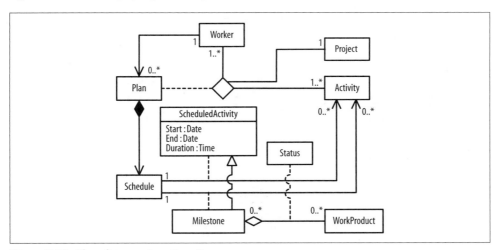

Figure B-13. Class diagram (question 4)

6. The following describes the figure:

- There is one type, named TDocumentation.

- There are two interfaces, named IView and IPrint. The IView interface has two operations, named show and hide, which receive no parameters and return a Boolean value. The IPrint interface has one operation, named print, which receives one parameter and returns a Boolean value. The print operation receives a parameter, named thePrinter, which is input and may not be modified by the operation, holds a value of type Printer, and is not initialized to any value.

- There is one implementation class, named Artifact.

- There are two undifferentiated classes, named Report and Printer.

Figure B-17 shows the resulting diagram, which includes all the steps in this question.

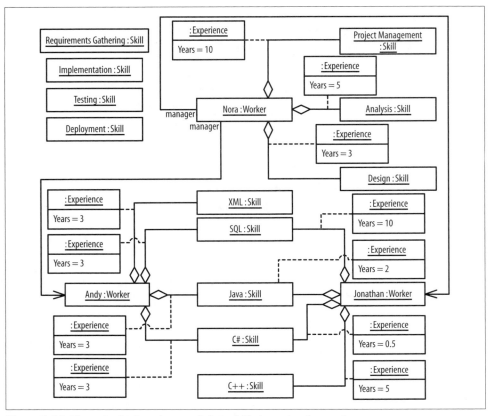

Figure B-14. Nora, Andy, Jonathan, and their skills (question 5 part a)

7. The figure shows a security subsystem, named Security, which has the following specification elements:

- An operation, named start, which receives no parameters and returns a Boolean value.

- An operation, named stop, which receives no parameters and returns a Boolean value.

- A Login use case that is realized by the SecurityManager class.

- An IUserManagement interface.

- An ISecureResourceManagement interface.

- An ISecurity interface that specifies an operation, named validate-UserNameAndPassword, which receives two parameters and returns a Boolean value. The first parameter is named theUserName, which is input and may not be modified by the operation, holds a string value, and is not initialized to any value. The second parameter is named thePassword, which is input and may not be modified by the operation, holds a string value, and is not initialized to any value.

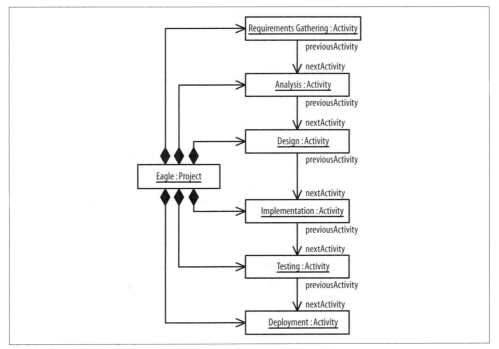

Figure B-15. The Eagle project (question 5 part b)

The subsystem has the following realization elements:

- A SecurityManager class that offers the start and stop operations.
- The SecurityManager class also realizes the Login use case.

8. Figure B-18 shows the resulting diagram.

Chapter 4, *Use-Case Diagrams*

1. The following describes the figure:

- The project management system interacts with human resources, printers, project web servers, and backup systems. Human resources include project managers, resource managers, and system administrators.
- A human resource may log in and out of the system.
- A project manager may manage projects, including maintaining projects, activities, and tasks.
- A project manager may publish project status by either generating a report involving a printer or generating a web site involving a project web server.

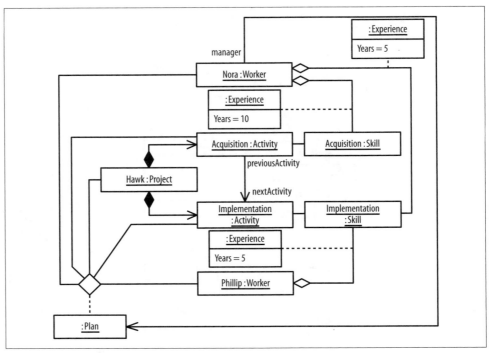

Figure B-16. The Hawk project (question 5 part c)

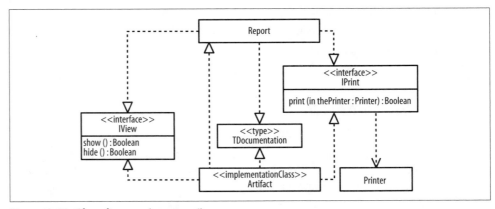

Figure B-17. Class diagram (question 6)

- A system administrator may administer the system, including starting up or shutting down the system. Before starting up the system, the system administrator may restore data; after shutting down the system, the system administrator may backup data. Likewise, the system administrator may initiate the process or the system may initiate an interaction with the system administrator informing the actor of the system's status.

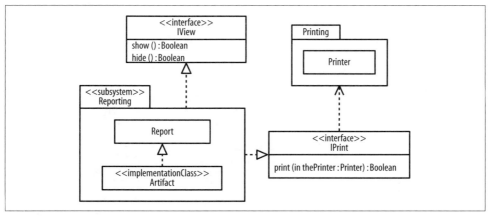

Figure B-18. Reporting subsystem (question 8)

- A resource manager may manage resources.
- When a project manager manages projects, a system administrator administers the system, or a resource manger manages resources, their activities are logged.

2. The following updates are made to the diagram:

   a. Figure B-19 shows the figure.

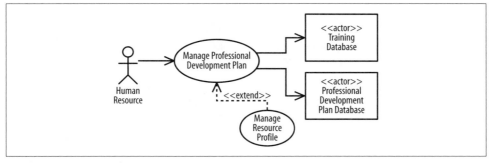

Figure B-19. Use-case diagram (question 2 part a)

   b. Figure B-20 shows the figure.

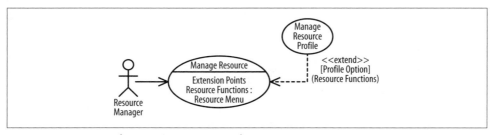

Figure B-20. Use-case diagram (question 2 part b)

c. Figure B-21 shows the figure.

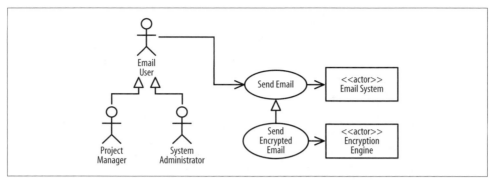

Figure B-21. Use-case diagram (question 2 part c)

Notice that a generalization relationship is used from the Send Encrypted Email use case to the Send Email use case, because when sending email and selecting the secure option, the whole interaction with the system is secure, not just the resulting email message being encrypted. If only the email message was encrypted and the interaction was not, this could have been modeled as an extend relationship from the Send Encrypted Email use case to the Send Email use case, and the Send Encrypted Email use case would have been named Encrypt Email.

d. Figure B-22 shows the figure.

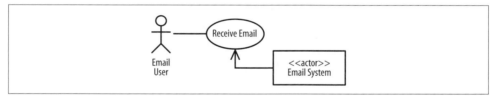

Figure B-22. Use-case diagram (question 2 part d)

e. Figure B-23 shows the figure.

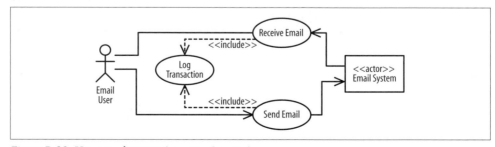

Figure B-23. Use-case diagram (question 2 part e)

Figure B-24 shows the resulting diagram, which includes all the steps in this question.

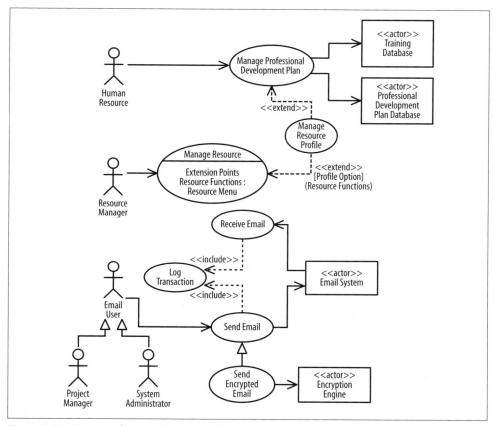

Figure B-24. Use-case diagram (question 2)

3. The following describes the rules for what use cases must be developed before other use cases:

- The Log Activity use case must be developed before the Manage Project, Manage Resource, and Administer System use cases.

- The Manage Project use case must be developed before the Maintain Project, Maintain Activity, and Maintain Task use cases.

- The Publish Status use case must be developed before the Generate Report and Generate Website use cases.

- The Administer System use case must be developed before the Startup System and Shutdown System use cases.

- The Startup System use case must be developed before the Restore Data use case.
- The Shutdown System use case must be developed before the Backup System use case.
- The Manage Professional Development Plan use case must be developed before the Manage Resource Profile use case.
- The Manage Resource use case must be developed before the Manage Resource Profile use case.
- The Log Transaction use case must be developed before the Send Email and Receive Email use cases.
- The Send Email use case must be developed before the Send Encrypted Email use case.

Chapter 5, *Component and Deployment Diagrams*

1. The following describes the figure:
   - The User Interface package uses the Utility package and the IBusiness Processing interface provided by the Business Processing subsystem.
   - The Business Processing subsystem provides the IBusiness Processing interface, uses the Utility package, and uses the IConsumable and IProducible interfaces provided by the Data subsystem.
   - The Data subsystem uses the Utility package and provides the IConsumable and IProducible interfaces.
   - The User Interface package, Business Processing subsystem, and Data subsystem reside in the User Interface component.
   - The User Interface component provides the IBusiness Processing, IConsumable, and IProducible interfaces.
   - The User Interface component is deployed on the Desktop Client node.
   - The Desktop Client node is connected to the Backup Storage Device node.
2. The following describes the figure: there are User Interface and Utility packages, and a Reporting subsystem that provides the IView and IPrint interfaces.
   a. Figure B-25 shows the figure.
   b. Figure B-26 shows the figure.
   c. Figure B-27 shows the figure.
   d. Figure B-28 shows the figure.
   e. Figure B-29 shows the figure.
   f. Figure B-30 shows the figure.

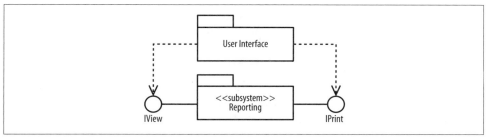

Figure B-25. Packages and subsystems (question 2 part a)

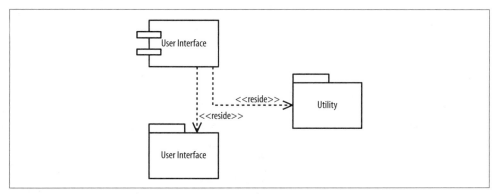

Figure B-26. Component diagram (question 2 part b)

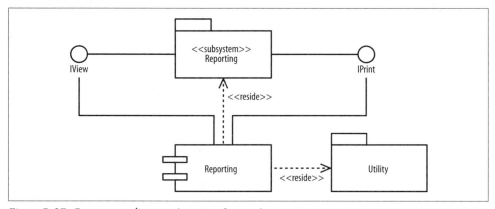

Figure B-27. Component diagram (question 2 part c)

Figure B-31 shows the resulting diagram, which includes all the steps in this question.

Behavioral Modeling

The next few sections present solutions for Part III.

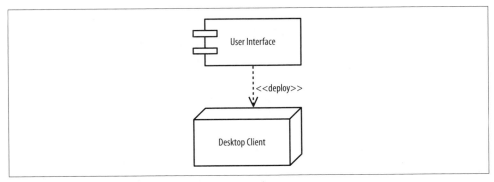

Figure B-28. Deployment diagram (question 2 part d)

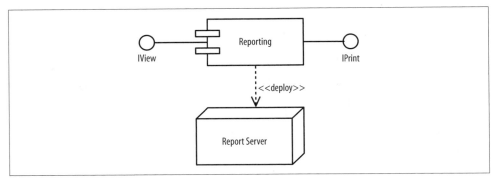

Figure B-29. Deployment diagram (question 2 part e)

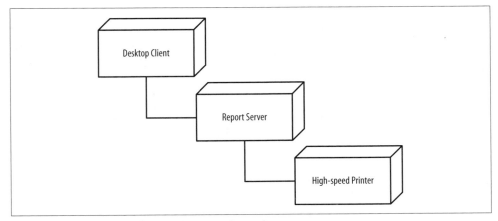

Figure B-30. Deployment diagram (question 2 part f)

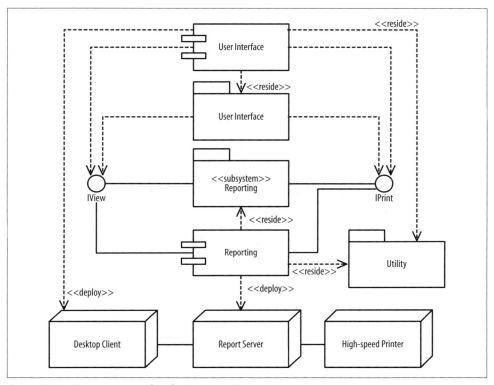

Figure B-31. Components and nodes (question 2)

Chapter 6, *Sequence and Collaboration Diagrams*

1. Figure B-32 shows the sequence diagram, and Figure B-33 shows the collaboration diagram. The interaction and collaboration is that of the Generate Project-Status Report described in Chapter 6.

   In Figure B-32, the following elements are missing:

   - ELM-01 should be:

     `4 : OutputData := FormatInfo (OrgInfo, PrjInfo)`

   - ELM-02 should be:

     `12 : OutputData := FormatWorkerInfo (UnitsOfWork, WorkProducts)`

   - ELM-03 should be:

     `[No more workers]`

   In Figure B-33, the following elements are missing:

   - ELM-04 should be:

     `[Populated Project] 7 : GenerateReport( )`

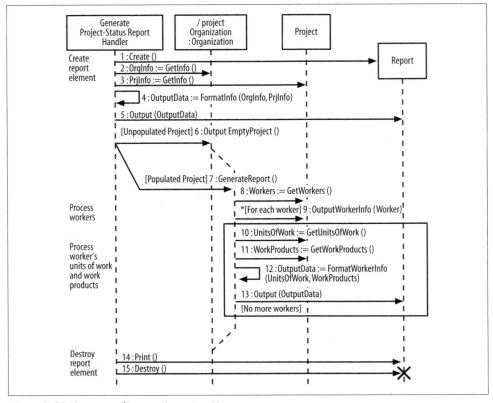

Figure B-32. Sequence diagram (question 1)

- ELM-05 should be:

  ```
  *[For each worker] 7.2 : outputWorkerInfo (Worker)
  ```

- ELM-06 should be:

  ```
  9 : Destroy ()
  ```

2. The following describes the figure: there are three elements, named Section, Report, and OutputDeviceInterface. The Report element has a Use relationship with the OutputDeviceInterface element and a Has relationship with the Section element.

Because these figures show an interaction and collaboration, each step adds to the previous step; otherwise, the notion of when a communication occurs would be lost!

  a. Figure B-34 and Figure B-35 show the figures.

  b. Figure B-36 and Figure B-37 show the figures.

  c. Figure B-38 and Figure B-39 show the figures.

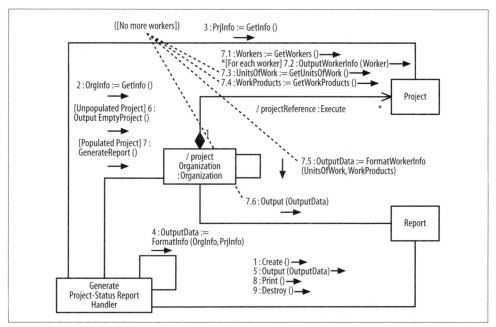

Figure B-33. Collaboration diagram (question 1)

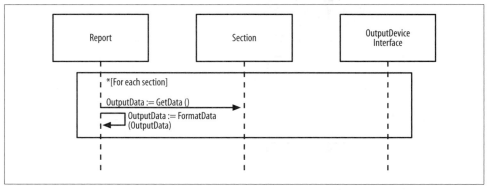

Figure B-34. Sequence diagram (question 2 part a)

Chapter 7, *State Diagrams*

1. The following describes the figure:
   - The Minimized state indicates that a window is displayed as an icon taking a minimal amount of space on the user screen.
   - The Restored state indicates that a window is displayed as one of many windows taking a portion of the space on the user screen.

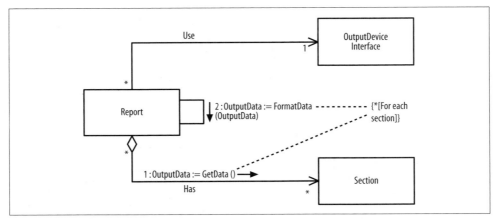

Figure B-35. Collaboration diagram (question 2 part a)

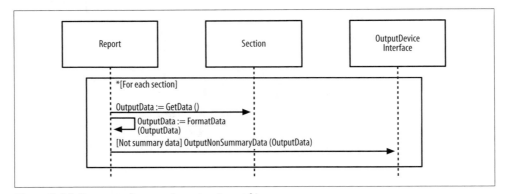

Figure B-36. Sequence diagram (question 2 part b)

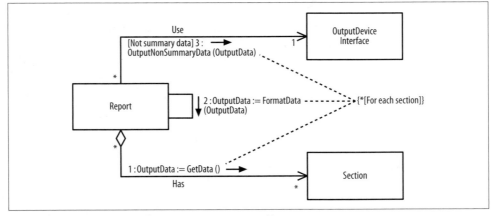

Figure B-37. Collaboration diagram (question 2 part b)

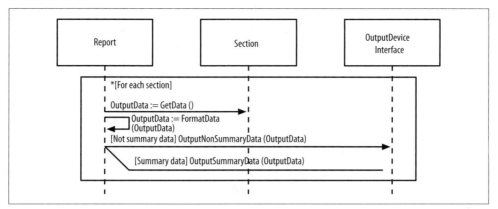

Figure B-38. Sequence diagram (question 2 part c)

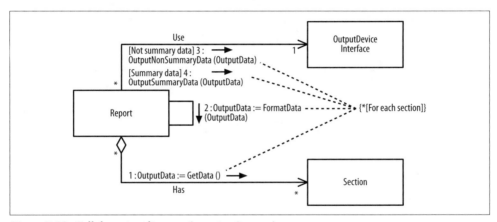

Figure B-39. Collaboration diagram (question 2 part c)

- The Maximized state indicates that a window is displayed as the only window taking all the space on the user screen.
- When a window is created using the Open event or operation, it enters the Restored state.
- When a window is destroyed using the Close event or operation, it may be in any simple state, including the Minimized, Restored, or Maximized state.

2. The following update the figure:
   a. Figure B-40 shows the figure.
   b. Figure B-41 shows the figure.
   c. Figure B-42 shows the figure.
   d. Figure B-43 shows the figure.
   e. Figure B-44 shows the figure.

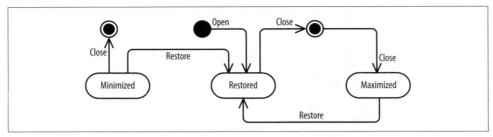

Figure B-40. State diagram (question 2 part a)

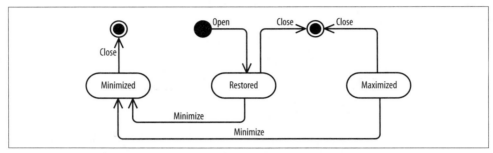

Figure B-41. State diagram (question 2 part b)

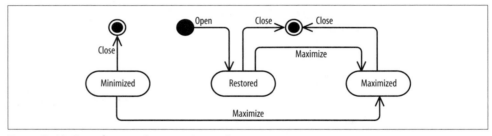

Figure B-42. State diagram (question 2 part c)

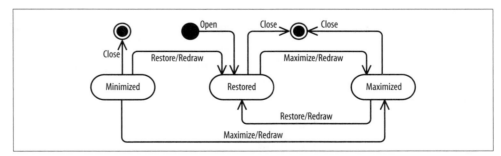

Figure B-43. State diagram (question 2 part d)

Figure B-45 shows the resulting diagram, which includes all the steps in this question.

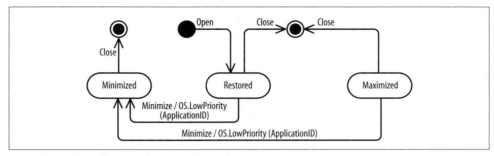

Figure B-44. State diagram (question 2 part e)

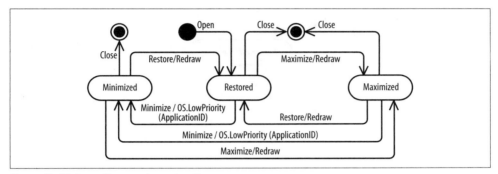

Figure B-45. State diagram (question 2)

Chapter 8, *Activity Diagrams*

1. The following describes the figure:

- The Project Manager swimlane shows the action states that are the responsibility of a project manager.

- The Project Management System swimlane shows the action states that are the responsibility of the project management system.

- The Printer swimlane shows the action states that are the responsibility of a printer.

- First, the project manager enters data using the Enter Data action state. Next, the project management system generates the report using the Generate Information action state. Finally, the printer prints the report using the Print Information action state.

- The Generate Information action state outputs a Report object and the Print Information action state inputs the Report object.

- After the printer prints a report using the Print Information action state, a project manager may choose to print more than one report.

2. The following update the figure:

    a. Figure B-46 shows the figure.

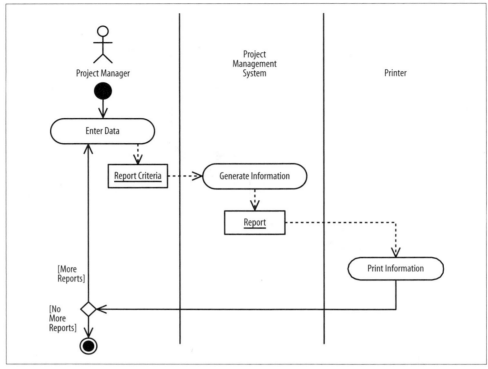

Figure B-46. Activity diagram (question 2 part a)

    b. Figure B-47 shows the figure.

    c. Figure B-48 shows the figure.

Figure B-49 shows the resulting diagram, which includes all the steps in this question.

Extension Mechanisms and the Object Constraint Language

The next few sections present solutions for Part IV.

Chapter 9, *Extension Mechanisms*

1. The following describes the figure:

- Organization is a stereotype definition that applies to classes.
- Made Of is a stereotype definition that applies to associations.

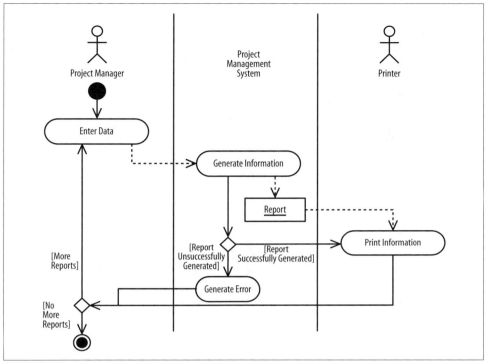

Figure B-47. Activity diagram (question 2 part b)

- The Organization stereotype has a tag definition named Name. This is a string that represents the name of the organization.
- The Made Of stereotype has a tag definition named String. This is a string that describes the relationship between an organization and the things that make up the organization.
- The Organization stereotype defines two constraints indicating that the name of the organization must not be an empty string, and that the organization must be made of at least one other thing (any thing).
- The Made Of stereotype defines a constraint indicating that the description of the relationship between an organization and the thing that makes up the organization must not be an empty string.

2. The following describes the figure:
   - The Business class is stereotyped as an organization using the Organization stereotype.
   - The Team class is stereotyped as an organization using the Organization stereotype.

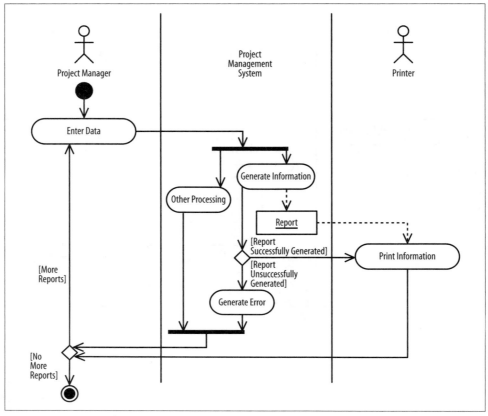

Figure B-48. Activity diagram (question 2 part c)

- The Business class is associated with the Team class in which the association is stereotyped using the Made Of stereotype.
- The Team class is associated with the Person class where the association is stereotyped using the Made Of stereotype.
- The Person class is not stereotyped.

3. The following describes the figure:

- Publisher is an object of the Business class and is stereotyped using the Organization stereotype. It has the tagged value of "O'Reilly" for its Name tag.
- Marketing is an object of the Team class and is stereotyped using the Organization stereotype. It has the tagged value of "Nutshell Marketing Team" for its Name tag.
- Production is an object of the Team class and is stereotyped using the Organization stereotype. It has the tagged value of "Nutshell Production Team" for its Name tag.

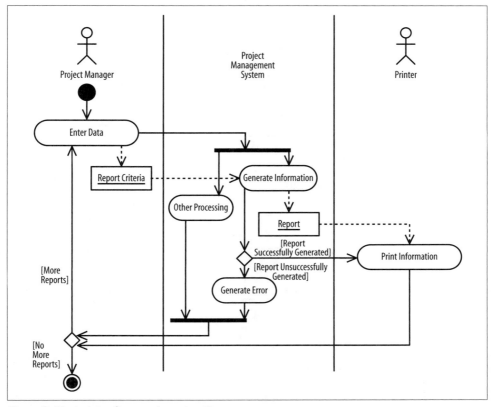

Figure B-49. Activity diagram (question 2)

- The Marketing object is linked with the Publisher object in which the link is stereotyped using the Made Of stereotype.
- The Production object is linked with the Publisher object in which the link is stereotyped using the Made Of stereotype.
- The Si object is linked with the Marketing and Production objects in which the links are stereotyped using the Made Of stereotype.
- The Jonathan object is linked with the Production object in which the link is stereotyped using the Made Of stereotype.
- The Andy object is linked with the Production object in which the link is stereotyped using the Made Of stereotype.
- The Description tag of each link that is stereotyped using the Made Of stereotype has a tagged value of "TBD" (to be determined).

4. The followingsteps show the solution:

   a. Figure B-50 shows the figure.

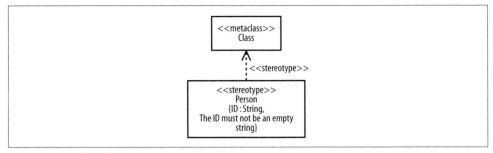

Figure B-50. Class diagram (question 4 part a)

b. Figure B-51 shows the figure.

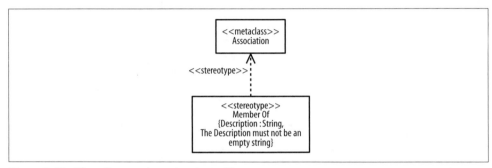

Figure B-51. Class diagram (question 4 part b)

5. The following steps show the solution:

a. Figure B-52 shows the figure.

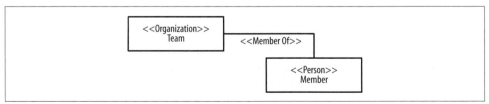

Figure B-52. Class diagram (question 5 part a)

b. Figure B-53 shows the figure.

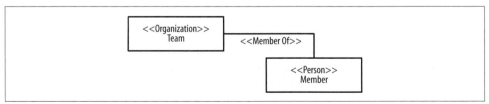

Figure B-53. Class diagram (question 5 part b)

Figure B-54 shows the resulting diagram, which includes all the steps in this question.

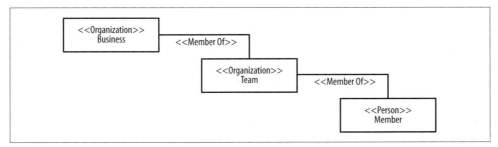

Figure B-54. Class diagram (question 5)

6. The following steps show the solution:

    a. Figure B-55 shows the figure.

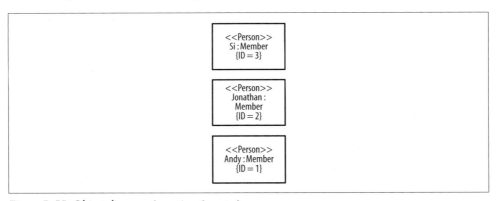

Figure B-55. Object diagram (question 6 part a)

    b. Figure B-56 shows the figure.

Figure B-57 shows the resulting diagram, which includes all the steps in this question.

Chapter 10, *The Object Constraint Language*

1. The following describes the figure:

    • The figure captures the relationships among and details about projects, plans, teams, people, skills, and people's roles on teams and people's experience with skills in the project management system.

    • A plan relates to a single project, a single team, and zero or more people who are human resources of the plan.

    • A project relates to a single plan and relates to a single team.

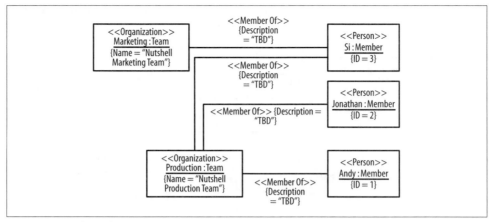

Figure B-56. Object diagram (question 6 part b)

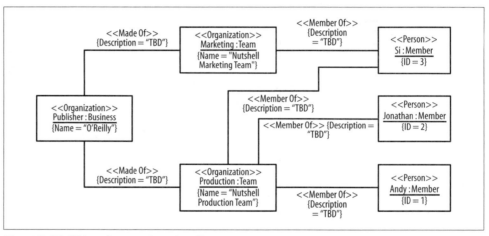

Figure B-57. Object diagram (question 6)

- A team relates to a single plan and relates to a single project.
- A person relates to a single plan.
- A team relates to zero or more people as members of the team in which a person plays a role. A person relates to a single team where the person plays a role.
- A skill relates to zero or more people and a person relates to zero or more skills in which the person has experience with the skill.
- A project has a name that is a string, a start date that is a string, an end date that is a string, a budget that is a real number, and two operations to retrieve the start date and end date of the project.
- A team has a name that is a string.

- A person has an identification number that is an integer and a name that is a string.
- A skill has a name that is a string and a priority that is a string.
- The relationship between a person and a team defines the title as a string of the role that the person plays on the team.
- The relationship between a person and a skill defines the years of experience as a real number that the person has with the skill.
- All the attributes and operations are public, but a project's start and end dates are private.

2. The following describes the rules:
   a. The priority of a skill must be one of the following: High, Medium, or Low.
   b. The budget of a project must be between 100,000 and 500,000, inclusive.
   c. The name of a team given a role may not be an empty string.
   d. The identification number of a person given a role must be greater than 0 and less than 9999.
   e. The identification number of each member of a team must be greater than 0 and less than 9999.
   f. The identification number of each member of a team must be greater than 0 and less than 9999.
   g. The identification number of each human resource who relates to the plan of a team must be greater than 0 and less than 9999.

3. The following expressions result:
   a. Within the context of a role, the following expression results:

   ```
   self.Title = 'Analyst' or self.Title = 'Architect' self.Title = 'Designer'
   or self.Title = 'Developer' or self.Title = 'Tester' or self.Title =
   'Manager'
   ```

   The keyword self is optional and the expressions on either side of the = symbol may be interchanged, but keep in mind this does not apply to > or < symbols, and the expressions on both sides of the or logical operator may be interchanged.

   b. Within the context of experience, the following expression results:

   ```
   self.Years >= 5
   ```

   The keyword self is optional and the expressions on either side of the >= symbol may be interchanged (in which case the >= symbol becomes the <= symbol).

   c. Within the context of a project, the following expression results:

   ```
   self.StartDate = self.plan.StartDate and self.EndDate = self.plan.EndDate
   ```

   Or the following expression results:

   ```
   self.getStartDate () = self.plan.StartDate and self.getEndDate () = self.
   plan.EndDate
   ```

The keyword `self` is optional and the expressions on either side of the =
symbol may be interchanged, but keep in mind this does not apply to > or <
symbols, and the expressions on both sides of the and logical operator may
be interchanged. Notice that the operations to retrieve the start and end
dates of a project may be used but are not required, because the rule is
expressed within the context of a project.

d. Within the context of a plan, the following expression results:

```
self.StartDate = self.project.getStartDate () and self.EndDate = self.
project.getEndDate ()
```

The keyword `self` is optional and the expressions on either side of the =
symbol may be interchanged, but keep in mind this does not apply to > or <
symbols, and the expressions on both sides of the and logical operator may
be interchanged. Notice that the operations to retrieve the start and end
dates of a project are used, because the start and end date attributes are private in the project and the rule is expressed within the context of a plan.

e. Within the context of a person, the following expression results:

```
self.team.plan = self.plan
```

The keyword `self` is optional and the expressions on both sides of the =
symbol may be interchanged, but keep in mind this does not apply to > or <
symbols.

f. Within the context of a person, the following expression results:

```
self.team.plan = self.plan and self.team.project.plan = self.plan
```

The keyword `self` is optional and the expressions on either side of the =
symbol may be interchanged, but keep in mind this does not apply to > or <
symbols, and the expressions on both sides of the and logical operator may
be interchanged.

g. Within the context of a project, any of the following expressions results:

```
self.project.plan = self.plan
self.project = self.plan.project
self.project.plan.team = self
self.plan.project.team = self
```

The keyword `self` is optional in the first two expressions but is required in
the last two expressions following the = symbol, and the expressions on
either side of the = symbol may be interchanged, but keep in mind this does
not apply to the > or < symbols.

Index

We'd like to hear your suggestions for improving our indexes. Send email to *index@oreilly.com*.

association ends, 58
  aggregation, 61
  composite aggregation, 62
  multiplicity, 60
  navigation, 59
  qualifiers, 62
  rolenames, 59
association roles
  collaboration diagrams, 138
  links and, 126
associations, 19, 28, 56
  association ends
    aggregation, 61
    composite aggregation, 62
    multiplicity, 60
    navigation, 59
    qualifiers, 62
  binary associations, 56
    interfaces, 72
    types, 70
  collaboration diagrams, 34
  communicate associations, 96
  communication associations, 116
  n-ary associations, 57
    interfaces, 72
    types, 70
  type-instance dichotomy, 20
attribute values, object diagrams, 29
attributes, 28
  classes, 45
    syntax, 47
  instance scoped, 48
  object scoped, 48
  object values, 54
  objects, 20
  simple constraints, 180
  structural features, 21

B

Backup Data use case, 102
backup system, 92
base use case
  extension use case, 99
  include dependencies and, 98
behavior modeling, 12
behavior sequences
  actions, 95
  interactions, 95
  use cases and, 95
behavioral architectural views, 39

behavioral features, 22
  classes, 44
behavioral modeling
  activity diagrams, 36
  collaboration diagrams, 33
  sequence diagrams, 32
  state diagrams, 35
binary associations, 56
  interfaces, 72
  types, 70
binary links, 64
Booch, Grady, 7
books, 192
business processing package, 81
business systems, 3
business-processing server nodes, 110

C

Cetus Team web site, 192
children, 74
class diagrams, 28
  association classes, 57
  associations, 28
  attributes, 28
  classes, 28
  n-ary associations, 57
  operations, 28
class modeling, 43
class roles, 125
  collaboration diagrams, 138
  sequence diagrams, 130
classes, 19, 28, 44
  actor classes, 92
  actor instances, 92
  association classes, 57
  association ends, 58
  attributes, 45
    syntax, 47
  behavioral features, 44
  collaboration diagrams, 34
  component classes, 109
  implementation classes, 70
    generalizations, 75
    realizations, 77
  node classes, 111
  objects and, 125
  operations, 49
    syntax, 51
  sequence diagrams, 33
  structural features and, 44

documents, 40
domains, 26
    contexts, 26
    domain elements, 26
dot notation in sequence numbers, 139
dynamic architectural views, 39

E

elements
    collaboration diagrams
        creating, 140
        destroying, 140
    sequence diagrams
        creating, 133
        destruction, 133
    stereotyped, 170
encapsulation, 24
enterprise data component instances, 110
environment model architectural view, 39
events, state diagrams, 149
    reset, 149
    severe error, 149
    shutdown, 149
    startup, 149
expressions
    constraints, 177
    OCL, 177–179
        contextual instances, 177
        invariants, 177
extend dependencies, 99
    extension point, 100
    extension use cases, 99
extensibility, 7
extension mechanisms, 167
    language architecture, 167
    profiles, 173
    properties, 171–173
    stereotypes, 169–171
extension point, extend dependencies, 100
extension use cases, extend dependencies, 99

F

final action state, 157
    activity diagrams, 36
final states, state diagrams, 36, 148
flow transitions, 157
four-layer metamodeling archtecture, 167
fragmentation period of development, 7
functional requirements, use cases, 94

G

generalizations, 25, 73, 102
    actor generalizations, 103
    ancestors, 74
    children, 74
    descendants, 74
    implementation classes, 75
    interfaces, 75
    parents, 74
    subclasses, 74
    super-classes, 74
    types, 73
    undifferentiated classes, 74
    use-case generalizations, 104–105
generic package, 80
generic-form interactions, 128
getDateAndTime action, 151
getters, 24
grammar, languages, 18
group business-processing server node
        instance, 111

H

has-a relationships, 61
history of UML, 7
    fragmentation period, 7
    industrialization period, 8
    revision period, 8
    standardization period, 8
    unification period, 8
human resource, 13, 92

I

implementation architectural view, 39
implementation classes, 70
    generalizations, 75
    realizations, 77
implementation diagrams, 31, 32
    nodes, 32
implementationClass keyword, 70
inactive simple states, state diagrams, 147
include dependencies, 98
    base use case, 98
    inclusion use cases, 98
inclusion use case, 98
increments, iterations, 11
industrialization period of development, 8
information hiding, 24
initial action state, 157
    activity diagrams, 36

initial states, state diagrams, 35, 148
initiator role, 123
instance scoped objects, 53
instance-form interactions, 129
instance-level collaboration, 129
instances
    collaboration instances, 128
    component instances, 109
    contextual instances, OCL
        expressions, 177
    interaction instances, 128
    node instances, 111
    use-case instances, 94
instance-scoped attributes, 48
interaction diagrams, 33
interaction instances, 128
interaction modeling, 121
interactions, 128
    behavior sequences, 95
    conditional, 96
    generic-form interactions, 128
    instance-form interactions, 129
    messages, 128
    optional, 96
    repeated, 96
interfaces, 71
    APIs, 71
    binary associations, 72
    generalizations, 75
    link ends, 72
    n-ary associations, 72
    user interface components, 109
    web user interface component
        instances, 109
invariants, 177
iteration, 10
    architecture and, 12
    increments, 11
    requirements and, 10
    risk, 12
    sequence, 10
    use case, 11
iterative approach, 10

J

Jacobson, Ivar, 7

K

keywords
    implementationClass, 70
    profile, 174

    subsystem, 83
    tag definitions, 172
keyword-value pairs, 172

L

language architecture, four-layer
        metamodeling architecture, 167
language aspect, UML, 4
language exstensibility, 7
languages
    alphabet and, 17
    grammar and, 18
    paradigm, 16
    semantics, 16
    sentences, 18
    words, 17
lifecycles, state and, 147
lifelines, 33
    sequence diagrams, 130
line paths
    relationships and, 17
link ends, 181
    aggregation, 67
    composition, 67
    interfaces, 72
    multiplicity, 67
        of 1, 181
        of more than 1, 182
    navigation, 67
    qualifiers, 68
    rolenames, 66
    types, 70
link objects, 66
    OCL, 183
links, 19, 64
    association roles, 126
    binary links, 64
    collaboration diagrams, 138
    link ends
        aggregation, 67
        composition, 67
        interfaces, 72
        multiplicity, 67
        navigation, 67
        qualifiers, 68
        rolenames, 66
        types, 70
    n-ary links, 65
    object diagrams, 29
local data component instances, 110
localization, 24
LogMessage action, state diagrams, 151

M

M0-level layer (user model layer), 168
M1-level layer (model layer), 168
M2-level layer (metamodel layer), 168
M3-level layer (meta-metamodel layer), 168
messages, 22
    clients, 23, 128
    collaborations, 128
    interactions, 128
    stimuli and, 128
    suppliers, 23, 128
meta-metamodel (M3-level layer), 168
metamodel layer (M2-level layer), 168
methodology, 6
methods, 6, 21
    information hiding, 24
    polymorphism, 26
    role identification, 126
model aspect of UML, 6
model elements, 40
model layer (M1-level layer), 168
model management elements
    packages, 80
    subsystems, 80
modeling techniques, 6
    state modeling, 147
models
    abstractions, 6
    behavior modeling, 12
    definition, 40
    structural modeling, 12
multiplicity
    association ends, 60
    link ends, 67
    qualifiers, 63

N

names, use cases, 95
namespaces, packages, 82
n-ary associations, 57
    interfaces, 72
    types, 70
n-ary links, 65
navigation
    association ends, 59
    link ends, 67
node classes, 111
node instances, 111
    desktop client node, 111
    enterprise business-processing server node
        instance, 111

group business-processing server node
        instance, 111
nodes, 32, 110
    business-processing server, 110
    communication associations, 116
    database servers, 110
    desktop client, 110
    printers, 110
notes, 38

O

object diagrams
    attribute values, 29
    links, 29
    objects, 29
object-flow in activity diagrams, 37
object-flow transitions, 159
object-oriented paradigm
    associations, 19
    behavioral features, 22
    behavioral modeling, 32–37
    classes, 19
    concepts, 19
        associations, 19
        attributes, 20
        classes, 19
        links, 19
        messages, 22
        methods, 21
        objects, 19
    links, 19
    localization, 24
    objects, 19
    operations, 21
    principles, 23
        abstractions, 24
        encapsulation, 24
        generalization, 25
        polymorphism, 25
    society of objects, 20
    stimuli, 22
    structural modeling, deployment
        diagrams, 32
object-oriented system, 27
objects, 19, 53
    anonymous, 54
    attributes, 20
        values, 54
    class roles and, 125
    classes and, 125
    collaboration diagrams, 34, 138
    lifecycle, 20

About the Author

Sinan Si Alhir is a practitioner (consultant, conference/public speaker, and published author) as well as an IT Project Management Certified Professional and e-Business Certified Professional. He has extensive information systems and technology experience, and breadth and depth in all phases of the system development life cycle. With experience in high- and low-level project work, and broad and deep knowledge of technology and methodology/process, he endeavors to deliver high quality, solution-oriented results within various application domains using a multitude of technologies and approaches.

He specializes in object-orientation, methodology/process, the UML, the Unified Process (UP), project management, process engineering, and various other disciplines, and focuses on empowering organizations to benefit from their applications.

Colophon

Our look is the result of reader comments, our own experimentation, and feedback from distribution channels. Distinctive covers complement our distinctive approach to technical topics, breathing personality and life into potentially dry subjects.

The animal on the cover of *Learning UML* is a kitten. Caring for kittens, much like caring for babies, requires a great deal of commitment, time, and understanding. It is much easier to care for a newborn kitten if it is still with its mother, as it is best for a kitten to stay with its mother for its first nine weeks. For example, it is very important for a kitten to be warm in the early weeks of its life. This heat is provided by the mother generally, as well as by its siblings, since kittens in a litter tend to huddle together. Kittens are born with their eyes closed, but they open after about seven days. During the first weeks of a kitten's life, however, it will sleep about 90 percent of the time. By two weeks of age, it will start to try to stand, and by four weeks, it is ready to walk and venture away from its mother for short periods of time.

If a kitten is orphaned or abandoned by its mother in the early weeks of its life, it's very important to monitor its care extremely closely. Keeping it warm and well fed is vital for its survival. It is a good idea to consult with a vet to make sure the proper level of attention is paid to the various aspects of a kitten's upbringing.

Mary Brady was the production editor and proofreader for *Learning UML*. Linley Dolby was the copyeditor. Claire Cloutier and Colleen Gorman provided quality control. Johnna Van Hoose Dinse wrote the index.

Emma Colby designed the cover of this book, based on a series design by Edie Freedman. The cover image is an original illustration created from *Old Fashioned Cat Illustrations*. Jessamyn Read produced the cover layout with QuarkXPress 4.1 using Adobe's ITC Garamond font.

David Futato designed the interior layout. This book was converted by Julie Hawks to FrameMaker 5.5.6 with a format conversion tool created by Erik Ray, Jason McIntosh, Neil Walls, and Mike Sierra that uses Perl and XML technologies. The text font is Linotype Birka; the heading font is Adobe Myriad Condensed; and the code font is LucasFont's TheSans Mono Condensed. The illustrations that appear in the book were produced by Robert Romano and Jessamyn Read using Macromedia FreeHand 9 and Adobe Photoshop 6. The tip and warning icons were drawn by Christopher Bing. This colophon was written by Mary Brady.

Other Titles Available from O'Reilly

UML

UML in a Nutshell

By Sinan Si Alhir
1st Edition September 1998
286 pages, 1-56592-448-7

The Unified Modeling Language (UML), for the first time in the history of systems engineering, gives practitioners a common language. This concise quick reference explains how to use each component of the language, including its extension mechanisms and the Object Constraint Language (OCL). A tutorial with realistic examples brings those new to the UML quickly up to speed.

C++ in a Nutshell

By Ray Lischner
1st Edition May 2003
840 pages, ISBN 0-596-00298-x

C++ in a Nutshell is a quick reference to the most important and most often used aspects of C++. The book's library reference is organized by header file, and each library chapter and class declaration presents the classes and types in alphabetical order, for easy lookup. Cross-references link related methods, classes, and other key features.

C++ Pocket Reference

By Kyle Loudon
1st Edition June 2003
144 pages, ISBN 0-596-00496-6

C++ Pocket Reference is a highly focused reference to the most vital and often-used aspects necessary for writing good, clean applications. Included is an introduction to C++, followed by short sections on topics such as classes, data types and memory management, with pointed examples and a brief list of tips.

UML Pocket Reference

By Dan Pilone
1st Edition July 2003
128 pages, ISBN 0-596-00497-4

An overview of UML, with concise coverage of case diagrams, behavior modeling, and UML terminology, plus a section that describes when and how to use a Use Case Diagram and what can and cannot be captured using it, is included. In addition, each UML diagram type gets its own section, showing the UML syntax readers need in order to use that type of diagram effectively.

Java in a Nutshell, 4th Edition

By David Flanagan
4th Edition March 2002
992 pages, ISBN 0-596-00283-1

This bestselling quick reference contains an accelerated introduction to the Java programming language and its key APIs, so seasoned programmers can start writing Java code right away. The fourth edition of *Java in a Nutshell* covers the new Java 1.4 beta edition, which contains significant changes from the 1.3 version.

O'REILLY®

To order: 800-998-9938 • *order@oreilly.com* • *www.oreilly.com*
Online editions of most O'Reilly titles are available by subscription at *safari.oreilly.com*
Also available at most retail and online bookstores.

C and C++ Programming

Practical C++ Programming, 2nd Edition

By Steve Oualline
2nd Edition December 2002
574 pages, ISBN 0-596-00419-2

Practical C++ Programming is a complete introduction to the C++ language for programmers who are learning C++ or transitioning from C to C++. In a new edition reflecting the latest changes to the C++ standard, this book takes a practical, real-world approach, placing a strong emphasis on coding style and the pro-gramming process. Readers learn not only the syntax of C++, but also how to write clear, maintainable code and to design and debug programs in a systematic way. For a hands-on approach to learning C++, this is the book to recommend.

Secure Programming Cookbook with C and C++

By John Viega, Matt Messier
& Zachary Girouard
1st Edition July 2003 (est.)
704 pages (est.), ISBN 0-596-00394-3

With a recipe box full of extensive code examples that developers can put to use in their programs immediately, this book serves as a code companion for those committed to making their programs secure. A wide range of security areas are covered, including cryptography (both symmetric and public key), random numbers, safe initialization, input validation, networking, authentication, access control, email, and anti-tampering.

C++: The Core Language

By Gregory Satir & Doug Brown
1st Edition October 1995
228 pages, ISBN 1-56592-116-X

A first book for C programmers transitioning to C++, an object-oriented enhancement of the C programming language. Designed to get readers up to speed quickly, this book thoroughly explains the important concepts and features and gives brief overviews of the rest of the language. Covers features common to all C++ compilers, including those on Unix, Windows NT, Windows, DOS, and Macs.

Objective-C Pocket Reference

By Andrew M. Duncan
1st Edition December 2002
128 pages, 0-596-00423-0

Objective-C Pocket Reference provides a quick and concise introduction to Objective-C for programmers already familiar with either C or C++, and will continue to serve as a handy reference even after the language is mastered. In addition to covering the essentials of Objective-C syntax, it also covers important facets of the language such as memory management, the Objective-C runtime, dynamic loading, distributed objects, and exception handling.

O'REILLY®

To order: *800-998-9938* • *order@oreilly.com* • *www.oreilly.com*
Online editions of most O'Reilly titles are available by subscription at *safari.oreilly.com*
Also available at most retail and online bookstores.

C and C++ Programming

Practical C Programming, 3rd Edition

By Steve Oualline
3rd Edition August 1997
454 pages, ISBN 1-56592-306-5

Practical C Programming teaches you not only the mechanics of programming, but also how to create programs that are easy to read, maintain, and debug. This third edition introduces popular Integrated Development Environments on Windows systems, as well as Unix programming utilities, and features a large statistics-generating program to pull together the concepts and features in the language.

High Performance Computing, 2nd Edition

By Kevin Dowd & Charles Severance
2nd Edition July 1998
466 pages, ISBN 1-56592-312-X

This new edition of *High Performance Computing* gives a thorough overview of the latest workstation and PC architectures and the trends that will influence the next generation. It pays special attention to memory design, tuning code for the best performance, multiprocessors, and benchmarking.

Programming Embedded Systems in C and C++

By Michael Barr
1st Edition January 1999
194 pages, ISBN 1-56592-354-5

This book introduces embedded systems to C and C++ programmers. Topics include testing memory devices, writing and erasing Flash memory, verifying nonvolatile memory contents, controlling on-chip peripherals, device driver design and implementation, optimizing embedded code for size and speed, and making the most of C++ without a performance penalty.

Mastering Algorithms with C

By Kyle Loudon
1st Edition August 1999
560 pages, Includes CD-ROM
ISBN 1-56592-453-3

This book offers robust solutions for everyday programming tasks, providing all the necessary information to understand and use common programming techniques. It includes implementations and real-world examples of each data structure in the text and full source code on the accompanying disk. Intended for anyone with a basic understanding of the C language.

O'REILLY®

To order: *800-998-9938* • *order@oreilly.com* • *www.oreilly.com*
Online editions of most O'Reilly titles are available by subscription at *safari.oreilly.com*
Also available at most retail and online bookstores.

How to stay in touch with O'Reilly

1. Visit our award-winning web site

http://www.oreilly.com/

★ "Top 100 Sites on the Web"—PC Magazine
★ CIO Magazine's Web Business 50 Awards

Our web site contains a library of comprehensive product information (including book excerpts and tables of contents), downloadable software, background articles, interviews with technology leaders, links to relevant sites, book cover art, and more. File us in your bookmarks or favorites!

2. Join our email mailing lists

Sign up to get email announcements of new books and conferences, special offers, and O'Reilly Network technology newsletters at:

http://elists.oreilly.com

It's easy to customize your free elists subscription so you'll get exactly the O'Reilly news you want.

3. Get examples from our books

To find example files for a book, go to:

http://www.oreilly.com/catalog

select the book, and follow the "Examples" link.

4. Work with us

Check out our web site for current employment opportunities:

http://jobs.oreilly.com/

5. Register your book

Register your book at:

http://register.oreilly.com

6. Contact us

O'Reilly & Associates, Inc.
1005 Gravenstein Hwy North
Sebastopol, CA 95472 USA
TEL: 707-827-7000 or 800-998-9938
        (6am to 5pm PST)
FAX: 707-829-0104

order@oreilly.com
For answers to problems regarding your order or our products. To place a book order online visit:

http://www.oreilly.com/order_new/

catalog@oreilly.com
To request a copy of our latest catalog.

booktech@oreilly.com
For book content technical questions or corrections.

corporate@oreilly.com
For educational, library, government, and corporate sales.

proposals@oreilly.com
To submit new book proposals to our editors and product managers.

international@oreilly.com
For information about our international distributors or translation queries. For a list of our distributors outside of North America check out:

http://international.oreilly.com/distributors.html

adoption@oreilly.com
For information about academic use of O'Reilly books, visit:

http://academic.oreilly.com

O'REILLY®

To order: *800-998-9938* • *order@oreilly.com* • *www.oreilly.com*
Online editions of most O'Reilly titles are available by subscription at *safari.oreilly.com*
Also available at most retail and online bookstores.